Praise for *If Darwin Prayed*

D1491408

"If Charles Darwin had not been in a spiritual muddle because of the inadequacy of his era's dominant theology, he might well have prayed with the power and passion of Bruce Sanguin. Some people dismiss Christian theology that embraces scientific evolution as arid. But they have not experienced Sanguin's deep, earthy, joyous prayers. The outpourings in this book shimmer with mystical connection. Their psychological insights elicit shudders of recognition. They offer direction for our sacred paths."

—Douglas Todd, *Vancouver Sun* spirituality columnist

"The emergence of evolutionary spirituality is one of the greatest religious advances of our moment in history. Yet it is one thing to embrace the truths of the evolutionary worldview and quite another to allow the spirit of evolution to transfigure one's being with its glory. In this inspired collection of sacred verses, arising from the depths of his mystic heart, Bruce Sanguin has given us precious stepping stones on the path to our own evolutionary awakening."

—Craig Hamilton, founder of Integral Enlightenment, host of *Awakening the Impulse to Evolve*, EvolutionarySpirituality.com

"My prayers are like meat and potatoes most days—nourishing, yes, yet rather familiar and routine, even when spiced with each day's particular concerns. The moment I started praying the poetry of this book, I delved into a box of chocolates—delicious and not to be enjoyed too quickly. Related words of scripture help slow the pace and encourage lingering in every liturgical season . . . Bruce Sanguin is speaking to our hearts and minds in fresh ways at a poignant moment in history, helping us move more fully into faith and science for the sake of deeper understanding, healing of creation, and sweet, honest prayer."

—Moderator Mardi Tindal, the United Church of Canada

"One of the great challenges, for contemporary Christians today, is finding inspiring resources that provide new language and metaphors to tell the Christian story from a twenty-first-century perspective. In Bruce Sanguin's newest book, you will find just such a resource. I am certain that once discovered, the poetic and touching prayers of this wonderful book will find their place in worship, in children's Sunday school classrooms, and in our homes."

—Rev. Dr. Fred Plumer, the Center for Progressive Christianity, U.S.A.

"As an evolutionary biologist who sees the universe as a sacred, self-creating living system, I thrill to the way Sanguin responds to the challenge of Rumi's God: 'Be very careful then, My servants, and purify, attune, and expand your thoughts about Me, for they are My House.' How could God *not* want humans to grow into ever-greater understanding of the magnificence of Creation through all the historically expanding capabilities of human minds and hearts? These inspiring prayers provide a new and heartfelt liturgical testimonial to the fullness of that Creation."

—Dr. Elisabet Sahtouris, author of *EarthDance: Living
Systems in Evolution*

"My favourite prayers in *If Darwin Prayed* are in the sections Season of Emergence and Season of Creation. These new additions to the traditional liturgy ring with humour, hope, and humility, revealing the Grace of unknowing, the scientific reframing of the Trinity, and Life's quirky strangeness. What's more, Sanguin's preamble to each section of prayers in this collection opens up possibilities, suggests new expectations, and deepens one's whole purpose for prayer. If Darwin prayed like this, I trust he would not only have voyaged on the *Beagle* but into spiritual discovery that would have renewed him every day."

—Dr. Marilyn Hamilton, author of *Integral City: Evolutionary
Intelligences for the Human Hive*

"Today, there is no shortage of wonderful books on prayer, but Bruce Sanguin blends wonder, contemplation, and Holy Mystery in prayers that resonate deeply with co-creators embracing their connectedness with all that is. These cosmic prayers for the liturgical seasons are uniquely inspiring for pioneers on the sacred path of conscious evolution, as the prayers evoke a coherence of heart, mind, and soul."

—Barbara Marx Hubbard, founder of the Foundation for Conscious Evolution, author of *Conscious Evolution: Awakening the Power of Our Social Potential*

"Until evolution and the new cosmology become the context of our faith, spirituality, and worship, the wonders of nature as recently revealed by science will remain intellectual abstractions. This is why Bruce Sanguin's adventurous new book is an important contribution to the current dialogue of religion and science. Surely the great geologist and spiritual master Teilhard de Chardin is smiling on Sanguin's work."

—Dr. John F. Haught, Senior Fellow, Science and Religion, Woodstock Theological Center

"The spirit expressed in Bruce Sanguin's inspired prayers is not just intelligent and innovative, it's juicy! It transcends the split between charismatic evangelical Christianity and better-reasoned but less-inspiring mainstream Christianity. The living presence of God shines through the words of these intelligent prayers. May that power help Bruce serve the birth of a new dynamic Christianity for a new millennium."

—Dr. Terry Patten, co-author (with Ken Wilber) of *Integral Life Practice*

"There are two ways to truly explore an evolutionary panentheistic Christianity. One involves a bunch of books with tons of footnotes and the other is prayer. Bruce's prayers are composed with the hand of a poet, the heart of minister, and eye-opening sincerity. You just can't help but lean into the integral vision they inspire."
—Tripp Fuller, co-founder of homebrewedchristianity.com

"Bruce Sanguin brings such common sense to these fine prayers. I thank God for the way Bruce thanks God!"
—Fr. Richard Rohr, Center for Action and Contemplation, Albuquerque, NM

IF DARWIN PRAYED

For Pam,

An evolving pilgrim,

Blessings

Bruce

If Darwin Prayed

Prayers for Evolutionary Mystics

BRUCE SANGUIN

Scripture selections throughout are from the New Revised Standard Version of the Bible.

1826 W. 15th Avenue
Vancouver, B.C. v6j 2m3

Library and Archives Canada Cataloguing in Publication

Sanguin, Bruce, 1955-
    If Darwin prayed : prayers for evolutionary mystics / Bruce Sanguin.

Issued also in electronic formats.
ISBN 978-0-9865924-0-9

1. Evolution—Religious aspects. 2. Evolution—Prayers and devotions.
3. Religion and science. 4. Spirituality. I. Title.

BL263.S26 2010   231.7'652   C2010-905392-3

Cover by David Drummond, david@salamanderhill.com
Design and Layout by the Vancouver Desktop Publishing Centre

14 13 12 11 10   1 2 3 4 5

To obtain digital or print copies of this book, please visit IfDarwinPrayed.com.

Dedicated to my daughter, Sarah,
my best case for a universe that is alive, ceaselessly creative,
and infinite in beauty.

*Every blade of grass has its angel that bends
over it and whispers, "Grow, grow."*

—The Talmud

Contents

Prologue

A colleague of mine once jokingly asked why I spend so much time writing sermons when I could spend that time looking for them. I probably wouldn't have written these prayers if I could have found them somewhere. But it's not easy to find prayers for worship and spiritual practice that are written from the perspective of the great evolutionary story of the universe. This "new" evolutionary cosmology has not yet worked its way into our theology, let alone our liturgies. I hope these are the prayers you've been waiting for.

For some time now I've made it a discipline to reflect on a weekly Scripture selection through the lens of an evolutionary Christian spirituality and allow prayers to emerge. I agree with Professor John Haught that evolution is Darwin's greatest gift to theology. Process theologians have been working to integrate the science of evolution with theology, but its liturgical integration is still in its infancy. This liturgical support is critical if evolutionary theology is to gain traction. These prayers are my attempt to put legs under this emerging theological model.

What was born of necessity soon became a weekly discipline of joyful creative expression. I wondered what prayers in support of the new cosmology and evolutionary spirituality would look and feel like: How would we pray together if we took the science of evolution and the new cosmology seriously—if we saw the presence we call God intimately involved with the modern scientific realities of the universe, the planet, and human beings? How do we translate Paul's intuition of a Christ who is cosmic in scope and sovereignty into prayer form? How do we pray into the mission that emerges when we bring this lens to bear on the text? What fresh insights might emerge from the ancient biblical texts if we brought an evolutionary lens to the task?

For most of human history the source of the mysterious voice whispering in our ears, "Grow, grow," could be attributed to God alone—for God was the source of all life, its creator and sustainer. Should "He" withdraw His breath, life would shrivel up and die. But then Charles Darwin came along about 150 years ago and empirically demonstrated that, in fact, nature could achieve this feat of growth quite well, without the help of a supernatural being. He even named nature's mechanism as natural selection. Darwin himself delayed publishing his research, knowing that his findings would threaten the very foundations of Christianity.

Which is exactly what happened with the publication of *The Origin of Species*. The first shock for many Christians was that nature actually evolves. The previously predominant view was that God had created a giraffe six thousand years ago with its long neck, spots, two knobs on top of its head, and splaying legs, all fully formed right out of the shoot. The second shock was the implication that we share a common ancestry with "lesser" creatures. Some of his readers took this to mean that humans are linked with apes and this was disturbing to say the least. (Nobody then imagined that our lineage extends back even further, to three-billion-year-old prokaryotic bacteria.)

The implications of such a radical kinship profoundly challenged the biblical injunction of the Genesis creation story that says humans should "subdue" creation. To acknowledge that the human being emerged out of the adaptive resilience and struggle of all of the creatures that came before us is to assume a more humble place in the scheme of life. Gratitude replaces arrogance as we realize that our challenge is not to have dominion over creation but rather to assume our proper place in our one Earth community. An evolutionary worldview implies an underlying shift in identity that can be perceived as a threat to those who cling to biblical literalism.

The shock still reverberates throughout Christianity today as fundamentalist Christians scramble to come up with scientific evidence for a "young Earth" theory and intelligent design. This attempt to turn premodern creation stories into factual, scientific accounts of reality betrays the original intent of the writers of these ancient texts: to help us connect with the ultimate mystery of creation. Still today, only 39% of Americans[1] and 59% of Canadians[2] believe in evolution. These results are strongly correlated to Christian beliefs.

My concern, however, is not with the fundamentalist strain of Christianity. Rather, it is with the liberal and so-called "progressive" Christians. We, who accept—and even celebrate—the scientific method and its findings, have been slow to incorporate the evolutionary nature of reality into our theology and liturgy.

We do not know conclusively if Darwin lost his faith because of his discovery. We do know that the theological models available to him were limited. There is no reason for the science of evolution and the theology of Christianity to occupy separate domains. We do not need to choose between the two, as recent scientific materialists like Richard Dawkins claim we must. Science and theology represent two different ways of knowing—one focussed on the exterior dimensions of reality and one that includes the physical world but also validates, celebrates, and develops the interior, nonmaterial realm of human experience.

As a minister in the United Church of Canada for over two decades, I have heard angels whispering in my own ear, "Grow, grow." Almost twenty years ago, on a silent retreat, I had a profound experience in which I understood myself to be the presence of the universe in human form. The dualistic separation between myself and the universe collapsed. I wasn't here as a visitor to a strange and alien pre-existing cosmos, I was its native expression.

---

1. Frank Newport, "On Darwin's Birthday, Only 4 in 10 Believe in Evolution," Gallup, http://www.gallup.com/poll/114544/Darwin-Birthday-Believe -Evolution.aspx.

2. Angus Reid Strategies, "Creation Museum Opens: Do Canadians Believe in Evolution or Creationism?" Angus Reid Strategies, http://www.angus -reid.com/uppdf/ARS_Evo_Cre.pdf.

I realized that, after 13.7 billion years, the universe had coalesced in form and consciousness in my own being. I was a product of the evolutionary process of the cosmos. More than that, the universe was continuing its evolutionary unfolding in and through me. My identity shifted from a very small and buffered sense of myself to a self-image as large and unified as the universe itself. (At this point in the story, my wife always reminds me that this kind of talk sounds outrageously narcissistic unless I point out that this universal identity is also true of every reader of this sentence!) Interestingly, though, it was this experience of realizing my larger cosmic identity that was the surest remedy for my narcissism. My little self (ego) was swallowed up by a more expansive identity: my evolutionary soul that was cosmic in scope. The concerns of my little self didn't disappear, but they were placed in proper perspective. Most importantly, from this state of unified consciousness I could see that indeed, as the prophet Isaiah said, the whole Earth was filled with God's glory (Isaiah 6:6).

I awoke to a universe that was alive in me and animated by Spirit. The mandate to "grow," to evolve, is an irreducible dimension of the universe. When we pay close attention to this cosmic impulse to evolve, and consciously consent to its influence and power, we awaken to a dimension of ourselves that the ancients called our soul. We discover our intrinsic purpose, one that is soul-sized, and we gain the desire and capacity to be centres of a sacred evolutionary impulse to create the future that Jesus called the kin(g)dom of God. Our creative self-expression becomes a moral imperative from the perspective of this big self. In and through this self-expression we discover that the future is within us.

Within the miracle of a living and evolving universe, our understanding evolves regarding God, the Christ, Jesus of Nazareth, what it means to be a faith community, and what it means to be human. There is no final, unchanging form of Christianity. God's last word was not uttered two thousand years ago in Nazareth. We can detect in the pattern of Jesus' life, death, and in the stories of His resurrection, the evolutionary bias of an eternal, loving Presence. The failure to update our theological and liturgical models has resulted in modes of worship, spiritual practice, and images of God, that are out of sync with reality (and Reality) as we know it to be.

Updating Our Image of God

God comes to you in whatever image you have been able to form of Him. The wiser and broader and more gorgeous the image, the more the grace and power can flow from the Throne into your heart. God is saying . . . "Be very careful then, My servants, and purify, attune, and expand your thoughts about Me, for they are My House."

—Rumi[3]

What if our images of God were informed by evolution as both a biological and spiritual impulse? The great story of the universe reveals that there is no disconnection anywhere in the universe. We are cousins with stars, giraffes, amoebas, bananas—let alone monkeys! We share an unbroken lineage with all of life. To modify the central image of Jesus' teaching, we are kin with all that is in the kin-dom of God. This is a stunning revelation. Mystics have intuited it, but now science has revealed it to be fact. We share a single energy with every form and every mode of consciousness in the universe. This knowledge should be the cause for great celebration in our churches every Sunday and in our prayer life throughout the week. As it turns out, the opening line of the United Church of Canada's creed is scientifically accurate *and* spiritually true: "We are not alone." There are no strangers in this awesome cosmos, just relatives. The illusion of separateness is just that—an illusion reinforced by a modernist ideology of materialism.

The congregation I have been serving in Vancouver has been encouraging me for years to make these prayers available to a wider audience. This collection is my way of listening to the whispering of the angels of Canadian Memorial United Church in Vancouver, British Columbia.

---

3. Andrew Harvey, trans., *Light upon Light: Inspirations from Rumi* (New York: Jeremy P. Tarcher/Penguin, 1996), 131.

This community has made their core purpose to "teach and practice evolutionary Christian spirituality," and I want to thank them for their courage and their willingness to experiment with seeing and practicing the Christian faith through an evolutionary lens. Evolution is all about adapting to changing life conditions. And conditions have indeed changed in our neck of the woods. Our church is located in a neighbourhood that boasts the highest percentage of people in the world who claim no religious affiliation. Mention the word *Christ* out loud in a local Starbucks and watch it empty. Part of this aversion to Christianity is due, of course, to a chequered history with violence and rigid belief systems.

We can't do much about the past. But it is my experience that when these intrepid souls discover that there is a community that is taking the discoveries of science and integrating them with our own rich wisdom tradition, they are willing to give us half a chance. Very often, their early impressions come through a Sunday morning service. These savvy visitors pay attention to the language of the prayers and the cosmology reflected in the hymns. If the prayers reflect a three-tiered universe (hell below, Earth, and heaven above) with a mythical God living outside the universe, intervening every now and then to straighten us out and then return to an extra-cosmic throne, it's not likely we'll see them again. If they hear "God *sent* Jesus to Earth," as though Jesus were beamed down from heaven to teach us a thing or two—as opposed to his existence being a brilliant occasion of this sacred, emergent universe awakening to itself—the chances of them returning are slim to none.

The prayers in this collection were written primarily as Prayers of Opening for Sunday worship—intended for unison prayer. If we're going to continue to pray this way, then the prayers should at least flow easily. The cadence and rhythm of the prayers reflect my attempt to facilitate this kind of unison prayer.

Canadian Memorial follows the lectionary—a three-year cycle of Scripture readings—so the themes are often inspired by the assigned Sunday readings. But in each instance, I interpret the text through an evolutionary lens.

Worship leaders may simply want to copy and paste a prayer into their weekly bulletin. You might be inspired by an image or a phrase and feel moved to expand upon it using words that are relevant for your context. Please feel free to use these prayers in any way that works for you.

These prayers also stand alone as meditations for private prayer. I was surprised to discover that people were taking the Sunday prayer home with them and praying with it for the whole week. The prayers here form the foundation of a spiritual practice. Although they are written in the collective voice, many people simply translate "us" and "we" into the first-person singular. These practitioners take an image or a single line from the prayer and use an ancient form of prayer called *lectio divina*. They allow the prayer, in effect, to read *them* throughout their daily activity by pondering the images, feelings, and thoughts it evokes.

The Three Faces of God

Just a quick note about the God I am addressing in these prayers. The American philosopher and founder of Integral Philosophy, Ken Wilber, helped me to see and validate what he calls the three faces of God or the 1-2-3 of God. God emerges in the consciousness of human beings and through these three faces: In the first person, God is experienced as the Great I Am, the God of all mystical traditions who is experienced as the deepest dimension of one's own being. In the second person, God appears as the Great I-Thou, as the Beloved Other before whom we offer our devotion. Finally, God appears as the Great I-It, the great interconnected system of nature, Gaia, or Web of Being—the impersonal God. Sadly, many traditions, including Christianity, have privileged one face over the others and have actively attacked or suppressed the faces of God they each found threatening.

The reader may notice that many of these prayers—but not all—begin with the traditional (for Christianity) second-person face of God, referring to God as the Holy One. This is not because I reject the first- and third-person faces of God. Rather, this is simply an acknowledgment that the second-person face of God is the portal through which the majority of people in mainline Christianity will be able to expand into and eventually embrace the other faces of God.

This is not to say that I believe that God is literally a person when I call God "Holy One." I don't. Rather, it is an affirmation that God is personal. It has taken the universe almost fourteen billion years to arrive at the qualities of consciousness—compassion, empathy, freedom, and love—that we associate with personhood. It is only natural that we would apply a metaphor which attempts to express an astounding evolutionary achievement—personhood—to the Ultimate Source. God is more than we could ever mean by personal, and yet is certainly not less than what we mean by this metaphor.

In my book *The Emerging Church* I include two chapters that describe how our images of God and Christ will be translated through our stage of consciousness, or worldview. If a person sees the world through a mythic (or traditional) worldview, then he may interpret the second-person face of God (the Great I-Thou) as literally a man with a white beard in a long, flowing gown—in other words, as a person. This is the God that scientist Richard Dawkins is so hard on in his writings. I often wish that he would turn his considerable intellect to the God of process theology or evolutionary theology. This kind of theology conveys a more mature spiritual intelligence, wherein God is not considered literally to be a person, nor does She/He/It control the universe or punish sinners.

An Evolutionary Pentecost

I wrote this book to support a new revival for Christian spirituality—what I call an evolutionary Pentecost. Just as the church was born of a fresh movement of Spirit two thousand years ago, I am convinced that the science and spirituality of evolution have the power to revitalize Christianity. As we allow ourselves to be the face of the sacred evolution of the cosmos, we gain the power and the burning desire to actually cocreate and realize the future that can emerge within each one of us—what Jesus called the kin(g)dom of God. To consciously situate ourselves and our congregations within the stream of this evolutionary impulse is to experience Spirit in a direct and life-changing way—a mysticism for our age. These prayers are written for this new Pentecost.

Gratitudes

These prayers could not have emerged without teachers and mentors. I thank mathematical physicist and cosmologist Dr. Brian Swimme, who was the first to awaken me to my identity as the presence of the universe in human form. He changed my life. Brian often collaborated with geologian and Catholic priest Thomas Berry, who has been a light unto my path. I remain grateful to the prophet/mystic Matthew Fox, who has been beating this drum for three decades now. John Haught's theological reflections on God as the Future have also inspired me. Going back further, the writings of Jesuit priest and palaeontologist Pierre Teilhard de Chardin, who knew that science and religion were both sources of divine revelation, continue to inspire me. I am grateful as well to American philosopher Ken Wilber, whose book *Sex, Ecology, and Spirituality* first opened me to the sacred significance of the science of evolution and provided me with a map of reality that informs everything I say, see, and do. I also want to thank the good people of the EnlightenNext community, and in particular their leader, Andrew Cohen, from whom the phrase "evolutionary impulse" entered my vocabulary; as well, Craig Hamilton has emerged as a mentor and translator of evolutionary spirituality into spiritual practices for the twenty-first century. I am grateful to my friends and colleagues evolutionary evangelists Michael Dowd and Connie Barlow, who have given their lives to helping us see scientific fact as God's native language. Finally, I want to thank Don Beck, whose evolutionary model called Spiral Dynamics helped me realize the importance of the evolution of worldviews. Every word of these prayers owes its life to these great teachers.

Without the support and context of the people of Canadian Memorial these prayers could never have been written. I am fortunate to be in ministry with such a faithful and evolving community of souls.

It was a delight to work with such an encouraging editor. Sarah Maitland's intelligence, keen eye, and patience made this a far better book.

My wife, Ann, continues to be an unwavering source of support and encouragement. Our love is what keeps us evolving.

If Darwin Prayed

I wonder,
if Mr. Darwin had imagined
a God bigger
than the theist's puppeteer—
and less aloof
from nature's ways—
how he might have prayed.

I wonder,
if he had viewed the great march of time
with a mystic's eye—
as Spirit's unhurried play with form and function,
not creation leaving God in the dust
and pulling itself up by its own bootstraps—
if his heart might not have burned with faith.

I wonder,
when the push of Eros
and the pull of the possible
caused him to close the *City of God*
and leave the dreary seminary
to set sail on board his *Beagle* destiny,
if he ever imagined that he embodied Spirit's
irrepressible urge to evolve.

I wonder,
when he reflected on the mystery of a finch's beak
and the glories of the Galapagos,
if Mr. Darwin considered his own adaptive brilliance
that brought forth *The Origin of Species*
(his great gift to theology)
an occasion of an even deeper Mystery—
evolution awakening in him.

I wonder,
if, hunched long years
over beetles and mollusks,
he ever considered
St. Paul's self-emptying God,
touching all with a rising,
noncoercive Presence,
and then going on ahead of us—
as did the Galilean—
calling from an undissected future,
beckoning this sighing creation
toward freedom and fullness of being.

I wonder, Mr. Darwin,
if your beloved Emma might have worried less
over your apostasy
if you could have played the prophet
and announced, with the Baptist,
that evolution was filling every valley
and making low the mountains,
preparing a highway
through Descartes' desert,
for the advent,
and not the end,
of God.

(If I were God,
I too would keep my presence hidden,
an allurement of love that predestines no fixed future,
conferring maximum dignity upon life,
as together all that is
joins in the great procession
of the formless, assuming forms most glorious,
crowning the human ones
with a distinctive diadem—
the capacity to select our own future,
naturally).

I wonder
if Darwin prayed.

ADVENT

Even though I'm Protestant, I've always felt as though this season is more about following Mary's example than it is about getting ready for Jesus' birth. After all, Jesus was born more than two thousand years ago, and while it's a good thing to retell his birth story, it strikes me that the deeper meaning lies with Mary and Elizabeth. I'm interested in how they came to believe that they had a central role to play in the birth of the sacred. This is a season of profound interior contemplation, during which we ponder, with Mary, "all these things" in our heart—in particular, that the Holy would choose us as vessels of the sacred, evolutionary unfolding of the cosmos.

Do we actually believe we have a role to play in the spiritual evolution of the universe? Mary's "yes" to the invitation of the angel invites us all to listen for the angel's whisper, and to not merely accept but to find our purpose in allowing our lives to be a womb where Spirit's dream for humanity—that all may realize the heart and mind of Christ—may gestate and be born.

The second predominant Advent theme is that of apocalypse—overturning an old reality to reveal a new one. According to the writers of the gospel, the advent of Christ, in both the "first" and "second" comings, ushered in an apocalypse. But today, we're better off not interpreting "the apocalypse" as a single cataclysmic event enacted upon the world by a God who wants to bring the whole thing to an end. God isn't about to destroy this precious world. Metaphorically, Advent is the season of preparation for the birth of a cosmological and evolutionary consciousness and worldview. As we open to this sacred birth, the result is apocalyptic, as previous cultural worldviews and structures of consciousness are transcended, yet included, in this ever-emerging evolutionary journey in and toward the heart and mind of Christ.

Mary's Song

LUKE 1:46–57

Magnify your goodness,
O Holy One,
through us—
as through Mary,
simple peasant woman,
your goodness was made known.

Lift all that is downtrodden,
within us,
and all around the world,
to a glorious hope.

Shake the dust of broken dreams
and dead-end futures
from the cloth of our lives,
and crown us with righteousness,
that we might be your people.

Bless us,
nurture the holy seed
growing within us,
that we might come to believe
the unlikely story
the angels told to Mary:
the life of God is about to be born—
in us.

Our souls magnify you;
our songs glorify you;
our prayer is a holy longing;
our life is a "yes"
to your invitation
to mother-forth your sacred future.
Amen.

Wisdom's Angel

LUKE 1:8–38

Come, angel Gabriel,
mute the voice of disbelief within,
and the voice of cynicism without,
telling us that we are not
smart enough,
important enough,
powerful enough
to birth your dream for creation.

Silence Zachariah,
inner priest of an old order,
long enough to rise above the narrative of diminishment,
so that the voice of Wisdom,
heard in the feminine conspiracy of cousins
and signalled in the leaping life of Elizabeth's womb,
may hold the talking stick.

Help us to hear Wisdom's wizened voice,
telling us how blessed we are,
with Mary,
to believe
that we, of low esteem,
are the lifted up,
enthroned and empowered,
appointed to birth Christ into the world.

We offer our song,
minstrels of the Magnificat,
and join our voices
with the mother of God,
magnifying God's holy name.
Amen.

Up and Becomers

LUKE 1:46–56

Cosmic Womb,
Universe Bearer,
Life of All Life,
Light of All Light,
Dark Mystery,
all creation magnifies
your holy name.

All creation rejoices,
with Mary,
that you choose to be born
and not remain Pure Being,
in her,
in us,
in this blessed realm of time and space.

You come to us,
and become through us,
in this evolutionary adventure of life,
divinity fleshed in a Bethlehem birth
but also in all willing souls,
who, with Mary,
and other up and becomers,
consent to give birth to you
and the sacred kin-dom.
Yes, we join Mary in magnifying
your blessed name.
Amen.

Taking the Plunge

MATTHEW 3:1–11

We gather at the shore of a new start.
John the Baptist is proclaiming an apocalypse:
reality shorn of pretence,
the facade of religiosity,
the clamouring for acclaim,
and the make-believe madness.
He stands there, dripping wet,
eyes of fire burning through the dry brush of our egos,
our half-hearted commitments,
and all that we've settled for.

Buck-naked souls,
stripped down and seduced by words of life,
we wade in,
reminded by John's uncompromising countenance
of what it looks like
to hold nothing back,
and wonder how new-born souls
behave in the real Spirit-drenched world.

"Bear fruit fit for the kin-dom,"
the Baptizer responds,
and everybody knows—
we know,
taking the plunge—
what is required of us.
Amen.

Overshadowed

LUKE 1:35

Overshadow us, O Holy One,
as your spirit overshadowed Mary,
announcing her role as a key player
in the Christmas story.

Overshadow our sense of insignificance
with the mystery that you chose us
to give birth to the Holy.

Overshadow our low estimation of ourselves
with Spirit's esteeming presence.

Overshadow our fear that you are calling us
with Spirit's empowering grace.

Our small selves relax
in the shadow of your grace.
We regain our full stature
and accept the leading role
in this drama of sacred birth.
We are reminded
that with you,
all things are possible.
Amen.

Advent Unity

ISAIAH 11:6–9

O Holy One,
in this season of Advent,
grant us the courage to hear the voice of the Baptist,
calling us to account,
insisting on more than talk,
on more than yet another workshop or conference
that excites our minds
but asks little of our hearts, our bank accounts,
or our lifestyles.

Give us the grace to repent, reorient, and recast
our daily lives according to the vision of Isaiah—
that prophet of paradise—
in which the ancient instinct to lash out
is replaced by a willingness to reach out
across our differences.

We enter now,
if only for an hour,
the kin-dom of peace,
in which the wolf and the lamb,
the calf and the lion,
the snake and the child
become fearless,
and we realize
that which we share in common,
with each other, with you, and with all creation,
encompasses and affirms the dignity of our differences.
Thank you, One in All and All in One,
for the promise of peace.
Amen.

Apocalyptic Awakening

ISAIAH 64:1–8

O Holy One,
we are a sleepy lot,
slow to stir to the calling of the cosmos,
deaf to the cries of Earth
and the forgotten ones,
human and other-than-human.

We distract ourselves
with trivialities that have become idols;
while the sun and the moon darken,
and the stars fall from the skies,
we are mesmerized by the market's alluring power,
eyes unflinchingly fixed upon the naval of our own net worth.

"O that you would tear open the heavens and come down,"
cries the prophet,
or at least tear open our hearts, pry open our eyes,
and end this slumber that blocks out pain,
but with it, wonder.

Our hope, O Holy One, is found in eyes wide open,
in hearts linked in common cause,
in small gestures of compassion,
and in alertness to your coming,
again and again.
As fire kindles brushwood
and causes water to boil,
so we await to be set on fire
with hope and gospel passion.
Amen.

Roadwork

MARK 1:1–8

O Holy One,
we confess that we have domesticated
and downsized you,
turned you into our own cuddly teddy bear.

But, along with our Sunday bulletins,
you pass out hard hats
and roadside warnings
that we are entering a construction zone
in preparation
for the Baptist's announcement:

"Every mountain and hill shall be made low,
and the crooked shall be made straight."

Keep us safe, O Holy One.
Even now, the dynamite of the prophet's proclamation
is lodged in the granite of our hearts;
O Holy One, break us open.
Let the roadwork begin.
Amen.

Daring the Dark

1 KINGS 19:9–12, LUKE 1:39–44

As the shadows lengthen,
we enter into a season
in which we dare to cross the threshold
into the dark.

Help us, O Holy One—
you who are discovered
in the silence of the cave
and the darkness of the womb—
to learn the mysteries of life
that are obscured by bright lights
and buzzing brains.

With creatures all across this planet,
help us to slow our heart rate,
lower our activity level,
and find a safe place
to hunker down
when all the world pressures us to hurry up.

Yes, in this Advent season,
help us to slow down for Christmas,
that we might attend deeply
to the birth of the Christ
within us.

May this be the gift we offer,
to ourselves and our loved ones,
as we wait in holy darkness
for the surprising birth of God.
Amen.

CHRISTMAS

It is significant that the central festival of the church focuses on a creative act: the birth of Christ. Creativity is a primary characteristic of the evolving universe. Christmas is a celebration of a particularly radiant birth, and this birthing process defines the very nature of our cosmos. Process philosopher A.N. Whitehead defined evolution as "the creative advance into novelty."[4] In science, novelty doesn't mean the latest, greatest thing. It refers to the emergence of a new form that is not only greater than the sum of its parts but also unpredictably new in a way that advances creation in the direction of increased complexity, consciousness, and unity.

The early church felt that something novel had occurred with the birth of Jesus. Using scientific language, we could say they intuited that the entire universe had coalesced in him, but something radically new had been added: he was, as the prologue of John's gospel puts it, the Word (or Sacred Creative Process) in human form. The one who was born of Mary would himself give birth to a new creation—a world shaped by God that this child, when fully mature, called the kin(g)dom of God.

But with a mystic's heart and eye, the celebration of Christmas is not merely looking back two thousand years in celebration of Jesus' birth. At a deeper level, we are invited to joyfully consent to the Word—the creative principle or sacred Wisdom—being born in and through us. We both give birth to, and are the incarnate presence of, the same sacred

---

4. A.N. Whitehead, *Process and Reality*, Corrected Edition (New York: Free Press, 1978), 283.

evolutionary wisdom that animated Jesus. In the words of Pierre Teilhard de Chardin, our vocation is to "Christify"[5] the cosmos in and through our very presence. To celebrate Christmas, then, is not only to celebrate the birth of Jesus but also to assume responsibility for this sacred birth happening in and through us.

---

5. Pierre Teilhard de Chadin, "My Fundamental Vision," 1948, XI, 191–92.

The Point of the Process

LUKE 2:7

Now, O Holy One,
we enter sacred time,
time suspended,
when history surrenders to mystery,
and we ourselves are taken in,
and taken up,
by a love story.

For this, the universe bursts into being.
For this, the galaxies shine—
lights strung upon a Christmas cosmos.
For this, supernovas make sacrifice
and our sun pours itself out
in the service of life.
For this, the march of life on Earth
makes its exuberant procession—
now present in lowing cattle,
in a single shining star,
in shepherds and angels,
and in proud parents—
to a Bethlehem stable.

And on this holy night,
no less,
does the cosmos coalesce in us
as we take our place
on the stage of sacred mystery
to celebrate the point of it all—
that you come to us
in self-emptying love
the moment we enter
the mystery of this Christmas birth.
Amen.

The Bigger Bang of Christmas

GENESIS 1, LUKE 1:78–79

Creator God,
from your fecund womb,
a birth-explosion of light and matter
erupted.
You declared it,
proud Mother,
to be good.

Time, evolution's handmaid, passed.
And from the depths of Earth,
you bodied-forth Jesus,
Spirit-filled and fired with holy vision—
some say a second creation.
A bigger bang flared forth in him,
Spirit's expansion in all directions.

Love burned in him so that our small
and isolated self might undergo a heat death,
birthing a supernova soul
and all the elements necessary for a new creation:
spiritual knowing,
compassion,
service,
and unambiguous consent to be future-shapers.

Our souls now see,
Universe Maker,
in this Christmas miracle,
the goodness of both creation stories.
Amen.

EPIPHANY

In Epiphany we declare Jesus to be the light of the world. Light is the milieu that surrounds and suffuses our lives, so it is easy to take it for granted. But artists have never taken it for granted. When the light is just right, a fence post becomes a sacrament of the holy. When sailors are lost at sea, they look for the beacon of the lighthouse to guide them to safety.

Scientists certainly don't take light for granted. The universe began as an explosion of light and heat that expanded out in all directions. Physicist David Bohm called matter "frozen light"[6]—light that vibrates slowly enough to assume form. The entire planet is reconstituted sunlight: certain cells learned to "eat" the sun through photosynthesis; animals then eat the plants, and humans eat the animals and plants. Everything we see around us, including our own lives, is a transformation of the sun's light, which pours out four million tonnes of hydrogen every second in the service of life.

No small wonder that Jesus came to be associated with light, the source of all life, the radiance that reveals the inner beauty of even the most mundane objects, the one who lights our path to the heart of God when we are lost, and the one who pours himself out completely and in awesome abundance in the service of the spiritual evolution of the universe.

In the human realm, light is often associated with conscious awareness. When we shine the light of consciousness upon previously unconscious thoughts, beliefs, and worldviews, we experience a kind of spiritual freedom. What was subjectively hidden to us becomes objectively obvious.

---

6. David Bohm, *The Essential David Bohm*, ed. Lee Nichol (London: Routledge 2003), 140.

Through the light of conscious awareness, we are able to see what had been shrouded in darkness, and therefore had power over the choices and the kind of life we could create. As teacher of divine truths, Jesus shone the light of his consciousness onto the realm of the kin(g)dom of God, an interior, relational, and social realm. By bringing to bear his enlightened consciousness, he revealed dimensions of reality that were always present but not seen by those who dwelled in the darkness of unconsciousness.

After years of contemplative and meditative practice, mystics describe experiencing uncreated light, the luminous presence of the sacred before the realm of space and time—of suns and planets—came into being. All light in the realm of creation is borrowed light. The Christian tradition claims that Jesus, the Christ, shone with this uncreated light.

Everywhere Light

MATTHEW 2:1–12

O Holy One,
what a confession that we cannot see
the miracle that is before our eyes.

We march to the drum of the dismissive voice:
"If you can see it, feel it, touch it—if it is located
anywhere in your small orbit of experience—
it is no sacred mystery."

Miracles, we believe,
happen elsewhere:
in secluded caves,
on mountaintops,
in the next town over;

and to other people:
to gurus and priests,
shamans and saints,
the gifted and great.

Forgive us
that even as we carry around
the entire universe in our bodies,
and in our luminous minds,
we look elsewhere for sacred revelation.

Forgive us:
despite knowing that each carbon atom in our blood
and firing neuron in our brain
came from ancient stars,
somehow we can ignore our own radiance.

Shine upon us, now, O Holy One,
that we might see your light
among us, within us, and all around us.
Amen.

A Mother's Confidence

JOHN 2:1–11

O Holy One,
the wine is running out.
The politics of spin and image
and mind-numbing superficiality
is depleting our collective spirits.
Our mouths are dry with cynicism.

O Holy One,
the wine is running out.
Our planet heaves and sighs
under the weight of our footprint,
yet her voice goes unheeded.
Our hearts are heavy with lament.

O Holy One,
the wine is running out.
A billion souls, sons and daughters
of mothers and fathers,
have not been invited to the party,
and "everybody knows."
Our minds are empty of solutions.

We turn, as did Mary,
to the one who makes room for all,
human and other-than-human,
at the banquet of life.
We turn to the one
who is a wellspring
of abundant life, with the words of His mother,
"They have no wine."

And from His heart there flows an unexpected abundance.
It spills over into our own,
and by the grace of Spirit,
through our own extravagant offerings of love,
we become living hints in a hurting world
that at this wedding of hope and possibility
the dancing has just begun.
Amen.

Christ, Luminous in All Things

JOHN 1:1–9; JOHN 8:12

O Holy One,
we dwell in darkness
when we are away from you:
ignorant of our true nature,
unaware of life's blessings,
disconnected and isolated
from the dance of the cosmos
and the blessing that we are.

We dwell in light
when we open to you:
aware that we are made in your image,
blessed by the opportunity of being alive,
at one with all that is,
enveloped by you,
luminous in all creation,
beyond all thought,
yet present in our "yes" to life.

May the light of the Christ
shine within us, among us,
and from us,
wherever darkness reigns.
Amen.

Send in the Clowns

JOHN 2:1–11

O Holy One,
what good news it is
that when the wine of abundant life gives out,
you find a way to keep the celebration going.

Just when we are convinced that the worst thing
that can happen is what always happens,
you send bright signs
that the party has just begun.

Just when we are happy to descend into despair,
you send in the clowns
and place party hats atop our frowning faces,
daring us just to try to not smile.

Into this world of wonder,
your beloved Cosmic Celebrant came,
with the last word on the subject—
silencing the political party poopers
and the religious prudes—
pronouncing blessing without end
and no good reason to stop the music.
Hallelujah! Blessed is your name.
Amen.

Into the Light

JOHN 1:3–9, ISAIAH 11:1–2

O Holy One,
we gather now to celebrate
that the deeper we go into the darkness,
the closer we come to your light.[7]

All manner of deceit will come to the light,
all corruption will dissolve in the light,
the lonely will be lifted into the light,
the poor and hungry will be radiant in the light,
the wealthy will be transformed by the light,
all confusion will untangle in the light,
loveless hearts will be warmed by the light,
even death will be conquered by the light.

By this light, all that is came into being.
Into this light, everything returns;
your divine glory shines out everywhere—
a wedding of flesh and spirit,
a celebration that must go on,
by the power of the wedded one,
dancing epiphany,
life and light of the party—
declaring for all with ears to hear,
eyes to see, and bodies that move,
that the best has yet to come to light.
Amen.

---

7. Bruce Cockburn, "Closer to the Light," *Dart to the Heart* (True North, 1994).

The Traveller's Homage

MATTHEW 2:11–13

We open now
to the way of the magi,
wise ones not afraid to journey
across the borders and boundaries
that mark the territory of the tribe
to what Spirit is doing in another country,
another tradition, and with other people.

We learn to lay our gifts before the Gift of God,
to follow the bright and beckoning star of our future
across deserts of unknowing,
mountainous obstacles,
and valleys of despair
to make an offering of our lives
to the "new thing" our God is birthing
in a land where we have never been.

And then, Holy One,
lead us back home on the path of the star-gazing sages,
choosing back roads and fresh vistas,
safe from Herod's hoard and the passport-phobic.
Laden with spiritual gifts—new sounds, tastes, and sights
of the star-blessed stable where you were born
and the beckoning mangers where you are still being born—
we discover that "home" is an expanding house,
as large as a cosmos,
as close as our hearts.
Amen.

Perspectives on Light

GENESIS 1, MATTHEW 2, EINSTEIN'S EQUATIONS

The ancient ones saw it this way:
in the beginning the Holy One allowed the light,
"Let there be light,"
and from Spirit's being,
a radiance emerged
that lit creation's path toward its sacred future.

The scientists see it this way:
in the beginning, from the darkness and emptiness
of nothingness,
an unaccountable explosion of radiation
expanded outward in all directions,
which now our instruments can measure.

The first disciples saw it this way:
Jesus, too, allowed the light
to brighten dark death's reign,
announcing a new creation,
brightened by justice for all.

The magi, lovers of the starry skies, saw it this way:
the heavens all pointed to an uncreated light,
now formed in a baby's eye,
Earth's native Star,
worthy of wonder and a gift-laden visit.

We might look at it this way:
that same light that shone in Jesus
shines now through us,
and this festival of epiphany is real—

or not—
depending on whether we allow
an eternal shining
to light our path
into a future that awaits
our distinctive stamp.

Let there be light.
Amen.

Deep Water

LUKE 5:1–11

We gather now
like fishers
with nothing to show
(or show off)
for our up-before-dawn industry,
except empty nets
and a down-on-our-luck mantra
that we're living into.

And so when a rabbi,
who knows more about wood shavings
than fish scales,
invites us to put out into deeper water,
it is respect, and not hope,
that gets us back in the boat
when we'd rather be in bed.

Through him, Holy One,
you invite us to put out
and drop our nets into deeper water—
where, far from shore, we risk the unforecasted storm.

"Go deeper," a voice as deep as our dreams beckons.
"Discover the abundance that is risk's harvest.
In vulnerability, discover love;
in authenticity, allow intimacy;
in commitment, welcome freedom."

Lead us, then, Lover of the Deep,
away from the safety of surfaces,
to drop our nets
into the dark and mysterious waters
of divine blessing.
Amen.

TRANSFIGURATION

Peter, James, and John followed Jesus up a mountain and there experienced his transfiguration. This uncreated light surrounded Jesus—the very light of God illuminating his form and consciousness. The story is told to confirm Jesus' unique identity and purpose.

From an evolutionary perspective, the entire universe is a transfiguration. All life on our planet began as a simple cell, and from this relative simplicity emerged what Charles Darwin called "endless forms most beautiful."[8] All that we see around us, including our own bodies and minds, are transfigurations of the originating Fireball. The entire universe is an ongoing transfiguration of the light and heat of the big bang 13.7 billion years ago. On the mountaintop, then, we can think of Jesus being bathed in uncreated light as the spiritual dimension of an evolutionary transfiguration that never ends.

---

8. Charles Darwin, *The Origin of Species by Means of Natural Selection* (London: John Murray, 1888), 306.

Light Transfusion

LUKE 9:28–37

O Shining One,
you are the flame burning within,
the beacon on the horizon,
the radiance in all creation,
the bright idea apprehending us,
the sparkling in the eyes of our loved ones,
the uncreated light that is lighting all.

Transfigure us, this very day,
as we open into the radiance of the Christ
in each other, in song, in word, and witness.
May this be the day of our enlightenment,
when we see with clarity
the sacred life we are called to manifest.

Remake us
as sacraments of the Holy,
that we might embrace our calling:
to see with new eyes,
reach out with gentle hands,
imagine with transformed minds,
be still with hallowed presence,
and be filled with grateful prayers.
In the name of the Transfigured One we pray.
Amen.

LENT

After his transfiguration, Jesus "sets his face toward Jerusalem" (Luke 9:51). This is code for Jesus' choice to face his inevitable suffering and death. In Lent we follow Jesus, knowing the outcome. This journey takes us into the heart of the mystery of suffering. Jesus continually reprimands the disciples for their refusal to accept that he must suffer and die. He tells them that they have their minds set on human things, not on divine realities. What does he mean?

Much of life involves ordeals—periods of intense suffering that are necessary to give birth to a new order, both within and without. When Anglican priest Barbara Brown-Taylor's husband reconnected with her after seven days of intense immersion in a Native sun dance festival, his first words to her were: "You make church too easy."[9] He had been through a spiritual ordeal that involved suffering. But this wasn't the kind of neurotic suffering that we bring on ourselves. It was genuine suffering in the service of greater personal freedom and power to align himself with divine reality.

We are often asked what we intend to "give up" for Lent. While this ritual can be trivialized, at its core it is a powerful spiritual practice. When we release our attachment to all that we believe is essential to our survival, we may discover that, in truth, they are addictions that are holding us captive, preventing our spiritual evolution, and stifling our capacity to proclaim and enact God's kin(g)dom. These addictions—to substances, relationships, and even the dominant stories we tell ourselves

9. Barbara Brown-Taylor, *Leaving Church: A Memoir of Faith* (New York: HarperCollins, 2007), 185.

about who we are—represent our neurotic suffering. Our genuine suffering involves coming off the addictions so that we can discover our essential spiritual identity: one with all of creation, one with Spirit, and called to use our precious life energy—energy that was being diverted to feed our addiction—in the service of abundant life and the spiritual evolution of our species.

The good news is that, as evolutionary creatures, we have the benefit of 13.7 billion years of resilience and the capacity to adapt to changing life conditions. Life keeps emerging out of cosmological and planetary cataclysms, such as supernovas, mass extinctions, and natural disasters. An ability to come through what the writer of Revelation calls "the great ordeal" is built into the fabric of our evolutionary soul.

Riding Wilderness Winds

MATTHEW 4:1–11

O Blessed One,
and Blessed Oneness,
we long to find for ourselves
the eagle's grace
to ride, effortlessly,
the thermals of life.

Distrust keeps the wings of our hearts closed.
We have been swept up once too often
by promises unkept,
by tragedies unexpected,
by twists of fate unanticipated.

And so, in this Lenten season,
we journey with Jesus,
Spirit-led,
into the wilderness of our apprehension
to face our demons of distrust,
and to find the courage
to lean once more into the winds of grace
and be uplifted by your mistral presence.
Amen.

What a Soul Seeks

MARK 1:12–13

O Holy One,
we can be a grasping, greedy bunch,
but you know better than we
that what we are reaching for is you.

Within the sparkle of diamonds
is the glint of your holy smile,
beckoning us toward true wealth.

Within the lure of gold
is your bright promise of spiritual wealth
beyond measure.

Within our fascination for power
is your alluring call
to discover the pearl of great price,
the life of spiritual wisdom,
to live in and as divine presence.

Help us to learn this way of the open hand
and the open heart,
to let the abundance of the universe
flow through us
and find its way back home
to your heart.
Amen.

Up from Eden
GENESIS 3

O Gracious God,
you have set us in this garden of life
and created us for freedom.
We seek release from this self-imposed sentence
that reduces "freedom" to endless consumer choice
and banishes us to the desert of anxiety.

We chase after the tawdry and transient,
while the simple practice of abundant life eludes us.
Captive to ego's petulance,
we focus on forbidden fruit,
flirting naively with desire's seduction:
just one more drink,
just one furtive glance,
just one more hour at work,
just one more deal,

until we lose possession of desire
and desire possesses us.

Drive us deep, Most Holy One,
into soul's terrain,
there to reclaim the gift of true freedom
that comes with gnosis,
a deep knowing of you,
hidden in the heart of the cosmos.
May the allurement of this sacred yearning
for union with you
lead us up from Eden
on this evolving journey.
Amen.

This Stepping Out

GENESIS 12:1–3, JOHN 3:1–10

Holy One,
we hear stories:
of Abraham and Sarah
loading up the U-Haul
with nothing but an old armchair
and an unlikely promise.
Is this the kind of stepping out
you ask of us?

We hear stories:
of Nicodemus stealing away in the night,
risking reputation and academic pride
for nothing more than a fireside chat
with a peasant rabbi
and a long-forgotten promise
reawakened by His presence.
Is this the kind of stepping out
you ask of us,
a walking away from the trappings of a life
toward the trembling Mystery of Life itself?

We confess, O Holy One,
an inclination to cling
to the self we have carefully constructed,
to the life we have inherited,
to the beliefs that keep it all going.

But sometimes in the night,
in the rare in-between moments,
the Life within our life beckons,
the Holy within the hectic quickens,
the Sacred within the scared stirs.

Help us to trust that the wind at our back
is your spirit,
nudging us toward the Nazarene,
in whom your promise
to the bold and open-hearted
is realized.
Amen.

PALM SUNDAY

P alm Sunday marks Jesus' "triumphal entry" into Jerusalem in fulfilment of an ancient prophecy: that the Messiah would enter Jerusalem riding on a donkey. Scholars point out that this kind of ritual
enactment of ancient prophecies was common practice. The celebration
is tinged with tragedy, however, knowing as we do in hindsight, and as
Jesus likely knew himself, that he was riding to his death.

From the perspective of evolutionary Christian spirituality, I interpret this event as Jesus consenting to the evolutionary pull of the cosmos
in fulfilment of his choice to proclaim and enact the kin(g)dom of God.
When the religious authorities warned Jesus to silence the crowds, he expressed a kind of evolutionary inevitability in his response: "If these people were to remain silent, even the stones would cry out" (Luke 19:39).
The people assumed their cosmological vocation of being the voice of all
creation when they declared that this one, who came in the name of
God, represented divine Reality (and not, by inference, Caesar): 13.7 billion years of creation had been waiting for this one to show up. And so
all of creation spreads its cloaks and joins in a canticle of the cosmos:
"Blessed is the king who comes in the name of our God!"(Luke 19:38).

Cheering on Wisdom

JOHN 12:12–22, MATTHEW 21:1–11, MARK 11:1–11, LUKE 19:28–40

O Holy One,
we come prepared to cheer on
our holy leader and hallowed child of Wisdom,
Jesus, the anointed one.

Our need is as great today
as it was for those ancient pilgrims
to honour and salute the presence
of truth and beauty and goodness.

For we have wandered far from Wisdom,
and we find ourselves cheering
for all the wrong things and all the wrong people.

Now we join in with this holy procession of hope,
that we might look into the heart of Christ
and see our own sacred heart reflected back,
empowering us to stay with Him,
and stay with our own deep integrity,
when the forces of chaos conspire to shake our conviction
and make peace with an unholy convention.
Amen.

Cosmic Procession

JOHN 12:12–22, MATTHEW 21:1–11, MARK 11:1–11, LUKE 19:28–40

God of galaxies and gerbils,
and this "gay great happening illimitably earth,"[10]
with great hope and celebration
we join the procession of life
en route to Jerusalem,
honouring the Christ,
in Jesus,
as alpha and omega.

The palm branches we throw down—
royal carpet for His passing—
are our own lives,
offered as hallelujahs
that it has all come to this:

Fourteen billion years it has taken
to come to this One,
arriving as servant, though honoured as King;
as peasant, though Lord of Compassion;
no formal education, though born as Wisdom;
dormant in the stars, gestating in the pregnant Earth,
and through Mary, Mother of God.

What joy is ours as we take our place
in the great procession of life,
heralding and blessing
this One who comes in your name,
and all who are coming
with a song of holiness on their lips
and a yearning for wholeness in their hearts.

---

10. e.e. cummings, "i thank you God for this amazing day," *XAIPE: Seventy-one Poems* (Oxford, Oxford University Press: 1950), 65.

Blessed,
blessed,
blessed
is this one who comes in your name!
Amen.

GOOD FRIDAY

The capacity of human beings to inflict suffering is painfully apparent on Good Friday. Jesus' execution was a violent murder of a good man. The crucifixion of Jesus represents humanity's rejection of Spirit, a rejection of the sacred impulse to evolve. If our spirituality is authentic and not merely based in false hope and optimism, we need to face our capacity to inflict great suffering and violence. In evolutionary spirituality, everything that came before us is gathered up within us. The cruelty and violence inherent in every holocaust exists, in potential, within us. To deny this is to drive cruelty and hatred into the shadow of our unconscious, outside our conscious influence, and therefore ready to erupt when we least expect it.

One way to understand our capacity for evil is through a metaphor from evolutionary science: The universe is comprised by what Arthur Koestler called holons—wholes that are parts of even larger wholes.[11] As wholes, cells, organisms, and individuals enjoy agency—they function autonomously to achieve their distinctive ends. But these wholes are also part of larger wholes, and as such, they exist in communion, serving the needs of a larger whole of which they are only a part. But when a part begins to function as the whole enchilada, without any responsibility or capacity to serve anything or anyone other than its own ends, you end up with a cancer cell. Over the long haul, cancer cells destroy themselves because they cannot function as a part of a larger ecosystem—but in the meantime, they are agents of death.

---

11. Arthur Koestler, *The Ghost in the Machine* (London: Hutchinson, 1967), 48.

The challenge Jesus put forth to the Empire of Rome, to his own disciples, and to us is to know the difference between serving God (the largest whole) and serving ourselves (the part that is currently living under the illusion of being the whole). Rome executed Jesus because he exposed their cancerous project of dominating rather than serving the world and God.

The human species is currently enacting the same kind of terror upon the left-behinds of the world, both human and other-than-human species. Animals like the Kihansi spray toad, the grizzly bear, the whip-poorwill, the Bengal tiger, and the sharks are going extinct because we have forgotten that we are a part of a larger whole. For three hundred years we have been in domination mode, unable to see ourselves as part of a larger ecosystem—our one Earth community. The ecological crisis is another crucifixion of Christ when we imagine Earth to be the body of Christ.

It is important to say, especially on Good Friday when we are contemplating the depravity of the human condition, that we are not *intrinsically* bad or evil. We are made in God's image, but we are living foolishly, and in need of a sacred Wisdom to remind us of our kinship with all in the kin(g)dom of God.

This Planet of Pain

MATTHEW 23:32–56, MARK 15:21–41, LUKE 33:26–49

Now we open
to the story of the Crucified and Risen One,
arms stretched out
across the chasms of fear,
pulling factions into his own broken body,
closer to his pierced heart,
so that this planet of pain
may one day claim as its own
the love flowing out from that
sacred, broken heart.

Yes, pull us in, Spirit of the Living God,
into the Heart of our hearts,
that we might once and for all
lay down our arsenals of fear
and take up our tools
to build the kin-dom of God
for the sake of all creation.
Amen.

Spirit's Cry

PSALM 22, MATTHEW 27:45–50

O Holy One,
be with us in this dark hour
as we face our collective shadow.

We do not do the things that make for peace
but rather do the very things that lead to violence.
We are slow to shed our ignorance
and quick to justify our foolishness.

Our planet joins our lament.
The lost souls of the extinct animals,
and those soon to be gone forever,
cry out this day with the Christ:
"Why have you forsaken me?"

The poor, the left-behinds, the humble ones
living in ghettoes from Rio de Janeiro to Calcutta to Port-au-Prince,
to the forgotten reservations of our own nation,
cry out this day, along with the Christ:
"Why have you forsaken me?"

May this story break our hearts,
our minds, and our spirits wide open,
that we might hear Spirit's cry:
"Why have you forsaken me?"

Help us to die with the Christ
that we might also be raised with Him,
and with all creation,
and discover our true nature,
one with your breaking heart.
Amen.

EASTER

As Paul says, the festival of Easter is an affirmation that there is a power at work within us that is able to accomplish exceedingly more than we can imagine (Ephesians 3:20). This power is at work bringing life out of death, hope out of suffering, and communion out of profound alienation. Resurrection is not resuscitation of a corpse, to be sure, but it is more than a metaphor.

The power Paul refers to is Spirit, the hidden order within the chaos, the life within death, the love and sense of belonging that is more fundamental than violence and alienation, and the creative impulse of the cosmos that is a first principle of reality. The first disciples claimed that Jesus was raised from the grave, and while we might not take the stories of Easter literally, neither should we dismiss their claims as an "idle tale" (Luke 24:11).

Paul himself was a powerful witness to the resurrection of the Christ. Paul underwent a significant metanoia (a conversion of heart and soul) after an encounter with a presence calling himself Jesus. He was convinced that the risen Christ had inaugurated a new creation—we might say the risen Christ was the firstborn of a new species of human (*Homo universalis*) with a new operating system or DNA to replace the clunky, old system. The gospel writers tell us that the risen Christ went on ahead of them, to rendezvous with them in Galilee. The risen Christ walks with us but also goes on just ahead of us, beckoning us from an unformed future to take our next best step. Galilee is different for each of us, but for all of us it is the launching pad for the new world we are called to cocreate.

Jesus' death and resurrection becomes a pattern for our own spiritual evolution. As we die to all the old narratives, beliefs, and assumptions that keep us attached to our small, egotistical selves, we are raised up into a larger, broader, and more encompassing Self—an Easter Self of cosmic proportions, motivated not by fear and mere survival but by the prospect of being an agent of sacred, evolutionary intelligence, capable of being a source of new life and the presence of a love that is always rising up in the service of life.

Save Us from the TRUTH

JEREMIAH 1:4–10, JOHN 18:33–38

O Holy One,
this search for truth
and its infinitely receding horizon
frustrates our need to nail it down.
Humour us, will you?
Freeze the horizon,
and fix a point that assures us
of truth's location.

Or convince us, once and for all,
that we wouldn't know what to do with truth
if we held it in our hands,
and remind us that whenever we try to nail you down,
you always rise up
and go ahead of us—
luring us toward the Mystery
beyond our intellect.

Grant us the grace of Jeremiah and Jesus,
who spoke not a word
until you had reached out and touched their mouths
with heart wisdom
capable of toppling empires
and raising up a kin-dom of "nuisances and nobodies"[12]
who concern themselves not with the truth
but with walking in the way:
lightly upon Earth,
humbly with all God's creatures,
and grateful for your holy company.
Amen.

---

12. Thanks to John Dominic Crossan for this image. John Dominic Crossan, *Jesus: A Revolutionary Biography* (San Francisco: HarperSanFrancisco, 1994).

Our Winged Hope

MATTHEW 28:1–10, LUKE 24:1–12, JOHN 20:1–10

O Holy One,
from the beginning
you gave yourself so that life might prevail.
You hid yourself in chaos
so that out of filaments of gas,
the galaxies formed;
from the death of stars,
new and necessary elements are born;
out of the fire of the sun,
a crocus pushes up through thawing earth;
out of the chaos and violence of injustice,
a wall is broken down,
a curtain pulled back,
a scapegoated prisoner makes a long walk to freedom.

And on this day,
we gather to proclaim that
from the tomb of violence, crucifixion, and death,
Christ sheds His grave cloths,
like a butterfly sheds a cocoon.

He emerges, our winged hope,
an elegant embodiment
of a new vision for humanity.

For you,
chaos and death
are but nutrients—imaginal cells[13]—
of a higher order,
a new creation,
an Easter re-formation,

---

13. Imaginal cells are the dormant cells within a caterpillar's body that emerge
in the transformation of the caterpillar into a butterfly.

which we could never imagine,
yet which is ours to claim—
a gift from an Easter God,
and an invitation
for us to spread our wings.
Amen.

Plan Be

EZEKIEL 37:1–14, MATTHEW 28:1–10, LUKE 24:1–12, JOHN 20:1–10

We open to you, "Ever-Present Origin"[14]:
bring us, breathing easy,
into the present;
rescue us from our anxious rehearsing of the future
and our gnawing away on the bones of the past,
that we might inhabit this moment
of our restoration.

Now,
we listen for the rattling of new life,
your spirit moving among the valleys of distraction,
weaving sinews of significance,
building the muscle of meaning,
fashioning the tendons of connection.
We hear the sound of our becoming
the resurrected body of Christ,
born of the union of desires:
ours, to be Christ's resurrected body in this age,
and yours, that we might find our soul's purpose.
We open to you, arising new in every moment,
our life,
and our hope in the unfolding future,
emerging from our deep commitment
to the present.
Amen.

---

14. Thanks to Jean Gebser for this image. Jean Gebser, *The Ever-Present Origin* (Athens, OH: Ohio University Press, 1985).

Planet B

JOHN 11:17–27, MARK 16:1–8, MATTHEW 28:1–8, LUKE 24:1–12

O Holy One,
we come this morning,
like the women on the first Easter morning
prepared to sweep up after death[15] and
to bring as much dignity as we can to the task:
we come to the tomb to make peace with "reality"—
a bruised and broken body,
emblem of the world, our planet, our dreams,
and the triumph of ignorance and violence.

Then word comes to us of an empty tomb,
of strange men, brighter than the morning sun,
announcing a new beginning,
a plan B,
a new creation—Planet B—
and that you, O Easter God, are doing a new thing.
We hear word that Christ has gone on ahead of us,
and now beckons us
from the rubble and ruin of our lives,
to put away our oils and ointments,
and to let the dead bury the dead.

We hear word of a future,
a future that we are called to create with you.
Christ is risen?
Christ is risen, indeed!
Amen.

---

15. Emily Dickinson, "Bustle in a House," *Poems by Emily Dickinson*, ed. Thomas Wentworth Higginson and Mabel Loomis Todd (London: Little, Brown, 1912).

A New Conversation

LUKE 24:13–32, MARK 16:12–13

O Holy One,
as the Risen One broke into the conversation
on the road to Emmaus,
so we ask that our discourse of despair
might be interrupted by a conversation of hope—
here this morning.

In the breaking of bread
and sharing of the cup,
warmed by the fire of each other's presence,
help us to recognize our Companion Host.

Help us to know that you are never finished with us:
in Christ we are ever emerging,
dying, and rising, with Him,
in faithful resonance
with the strange, intimate presence,
causing our hearts to burn with the hope
that the best is yet to come.
Amen.

Fresh Songs of Hope

LUKE 24:13–32, MARK 16:12–13

Living God,
break through the disappointments and disillusionments
that send us home,
sad and silent,
like Emmaus disciples
with crucified hearts.

You, who toss boulders from the mouths of tombs
like pebbles into a river,
touch us this day
with ripples of resurrection joy.

The news is too good not to be true,
that nothing in life or in death
can impede your vitality
from reaching and raising us
from death to abundant life.

In this time together,
help us to recognize the Risen One in our midst,
that our hearts might stir once more
with possibilities of resurrection,
and fresh songs of hope.
Amen.

Fire-Breather

JOHN 20:19–29, LUKE 24:36–43

O Holy One,
we confess conformance to this world;
Easter happened last weekend,
and already we're living off leftovers.
We have returned to our routines,
and locked ourselves into familiar patterns
as the disciples locked themselves
behind closed doors.

It is good news indeed
that there is no hiding from the Risen One.
He comes as Destiny's servant,
walking through walls of fear,
breathing the fire of the Holy Spirit
into our unbelieving hearts and
offering us a peace
which surpasses all understanding:
the peace of renewed purpose,
of a blessed unrest,
of realizing that the Easter story
is about our own resurrection after all,
and that there is work to done:
proclaiming God's love,
healing the brokenhearted,
speaking out for creation,
and above all,
opening to the evolving push and pull
of Spirit's call.

O Risen One,
breathe on us,
set us on fire and send us out,
that we might rise from our graves of fear
and go forth boldly as your Easter people.
Amen.

God Bless the Holdouts

JOHN 20:24–29, LUKE 24:36–43

O Risen One,
help us to tease out this sacred tangle:
you, in the Father;
us, in you;
all entwined by Spirit?
A holy braid, not weakened by us?

In fact, you say, a lifeline for the lost,
with the power to forgive sin,
to forge new futures not tethered to the worst
that has happened to us
but rather to the best that you have in store for us?

Forgive us if we, like Thomas,
hold out for just a bit
to touch the holes in your hands and your side,
and to take a peek where life's thorns have punctured our hope.

But there you are,
enfleshed in today's tortured,
in the left-behinds and the lonely,
and in our own refusal to give in to despair.

You rise up, again and again,
in the doubters and the holdouts,
who, more deeply than most,
want to believe in the power of resurrection.
Amen.

Busting Out

JOHN 11:17–27, MARK 16:1–8, MATTHEW 28:1–8, LUKE 24:1–12

O Holy One,
who gives life to the dead
and calls formless potential
into fullness of being,
we feel your tug to realize a resurrection.

Bust open the cold tomb of made-up minds,
massage our hardened hearts into supple softness,
grant us the mind of Christ,
and the courage of Spirit,
to become the people we were meant to be.

Show us where we have erected walls of fear
and convinced ourselves
that they are not only necessary,
but sacred.
Show us what we are pretending
not to know
on this sacred path of becoming.

We commit to revealing and realizing
your kin-dom,
in our homes and houses of parliament,
in our boardrooms and business deals,
in our policy making and in our peacemaking,
all in the name of the ever-rising Christ.
Amen.

Getting to Galilee

MATTHEW 28:1–8

We open now to the power of resurrection,
to the loving presence
flowing through the cosmos
and through us,
rolling away stones from the mouths of tombs,
rising up out of death,
faithful servant
of eternal life.

We open to the healing power
of our Easter God,
Hidden Wholeness,
weaving tapestries
from what we thought
were merely tattered and torn ends,
death's detritus.

The grave cloths lie,
emptied of form,
in a cave designed for despair
yet telling a different and deeper truth:
that death is but a portal through which
divine emptiness slips away
and into the future,
beckoning us to go to Galilee—
those places and times of our lives
when our hearts first burned with hope—
and await instructions for our Easter mission.

We find no good reason
to withhold our hallelujahs.
Christ is risen!
Hallelujah!

The Silence of the Seed

MATTHEW 13:1–9; MARK 4:1–9, 4:26–29; LUKE 8:4–8, 11–15

We are scattered now,
like seeds,
in the rich soil of becoming.

This breaking open—
of atoms, galaxies, and bacteria
into the next novel moment—
is beyond our comprehension.

Yet we know in our depths
that we are most ourselves
when we are in the breaking through,
in the sprouting life,
in the death giving way to new life,
in the holy mystery
of unceasing yearning to manifest.

We are this mystery of growth,
beyond comprehension,
and yet as intimate and personal
as our breath—
this incessant sigh for completion.

And so we keep the expectant silence of the seed
before the mystery of emergence,
knowing that you are the one
who makes all things new.
Amen.

ASCENSION

This is a strange story to modernist ears. Jesus promises the Holy Spirit to the disciples and then flies off to heaven to be with God. Premodern cosmology situated God beyond the dome of the skies that separated Earth from heaven—God's home address.

An evolutionary, developmental model can help. Ancients intuited that there is an ascending cosmological order from matter to mind to soul to spirit. There were problems with this model, however. For one thing, in these premodern models, God was thought to have established these realms for eternity, so there was no sense of an evolving reality. Between matter and spirit, there was an unbridgeable chasm. Within this model, people naturally wanted to escape the entrapment of this bodily existence on Earth in order to be closer to God in the realm of Spirit. This was the so-called Great Chain of Being.

However, if we replace the Great Chain with the Great Nest of Being, we can see that matter is not the lowest rung on the ladder but the exterior dimension of every level of being.[16] And when it comes to the non-physical dimensions of reality, the earlier levels of consciousness and cultural worldviews are nested within the levels and worldviews that emerge as humans adapt to changing life conditions. This is the evolutionary journey as it relates to the human species. Theorists and researches such as Jean Gebser, Clare Graves, Don Beck, Howard Gardner, and James Fowler have each confirmed these emergent waves of development. For simplicity's sake, let's just call the levels premodern, modern, postmodern,

---

16. I am grateful to Ken Wilber for this insight. Ken Wilber, *Toward a Comprehensive Theory of Subtle Energies*, Shambhala Publications, http://wilber.shambhala.com/html/books/kosmos/excerptG/part1.cfm.

and integral. Each of these worldviews is transcended yet included (and therefore nested) within the emergent worldview.

The later levels are not better than the earlier ones, nor are they closer to God. But, in response to new life conditions, they do make it possible to see reality through an increasing number of perspectives and with an increasing complexity. For example, if someone sees the world through a modernist/achievist[17] lens, then the integral perspective is above his or her head. An oil spill off the Gulf of Mexico, while unfortunate to the modernist/achievist worldview, is simply the cost of doing business. The loss of sea creatures, shore birds, and the pollution of the ocean won't be top of mind because an ecosystem's perspective doesn't emerge as a functional worldview until postmodernism. Therefore, the modernist/achievist will need to ascend the developmental ladder in order to see business itself as an expression of, and dependent upon, the larger ecosystem.

To ascend with Christ to the right hand of God means continually opening ourselves to the heart and mind of Christ as a source of allurement to more expansive worldviews and higher forms of spiritual consciousness. Again, "higher" simply means gaining new, more comprehenive perspectives on all dimensions of life and the capacity to respond with greater complexity. From a developmental perspective, this spiritual practice of ascension never ends because life continues to evolve, thus evoking new and necessary intelligences to live with maximum freedom and fullness of being.

---

17. See Don Beck and Christopher Cowan's model of Spiral Dynamics. Don Beck and Christopher Cowan, *Spiral Dynamics Gateway*, National Values Center, Inc., http://www.spiraldynamics.com.

The View from Thirty Thousand Feet

MARK 16:19–20, LUKE 24:50–53

This path of ascension,
prefigured in Christ,
lifts us up and opens us out
into vistas of self, nature, and culture
not visible through eyes of fear.

But Teacher's
leave-taking love,
his parting gesture of calling in a substitute Spirit
to fill us with power and fuel our own liftoff,
carries us into a holy orbit,
and with Christ we enjoy the view
from thirty thousand feet.

An awesome horizon rises up:
a new self, a new community,
a new Earth, a new perspective,
and a blessed confidence to walk forward
and realize
the ever-receding horizon
of the kin-dom of God.
Amen.

PENTECOST

Pentecost is the festival that marks the birth of the church through the outpouring of the Holy Spirit. This outpouring was associated with glossolalia (speaking in tongues). The local people thought that the disciples were drunk, but their ecstatic utterances served a purpose: visiting Jews from all across the Mediterranean basin who spoke foreign languages could hear the proclamation of the Good News in their own tongue. This reversed the story of the Tower of Babel, wherein God confounded the project of building a tower into the heavens by introducing new languages, and thus, the builders could not co-operate in their project of usurping God's role.

I am convinced that Spirit once again has a new story to tell—one that will issue in a second Pentecost and a new iteration of what it means to be the church. We are now learning the language of a new evolutionary cosmology, which is the context for the sacred texts of all faith systems and for secular culture in general. We now know that we all share a common creation story that unites everything and everybody. We are all manifestations of a single unifying event—magnificent in our diversity, yes, but underlying this diversity is a uni-verse, a single story that unites us.

The incredible diversity we enjoy and celebrate is contained within a unifying, sacred narrative. We are geologically, biologically, and spiritually one universe community. Biologist E.O. Wilson coined the term biophilia (love of life) and suggested that loving life in all its forms was the most important spiritual practice of the twenty-first century. Futurist Duane Elgin broadened this to prescribe cosmophilia, love of the entire cosmos.

But this new evolutionary Pentecost goes beyond just telling a new story, as magnificent as this sacred tale is; we can also tap into the underlying power and dynamic of the evolving cosmos—the evolutionary impulse to evolve—just as the first followers of Jesus tapped into a fresh outpouring of Spirit. In human beings, natural selection becomes *actual* selection when the conscious intention to create a new future awakens in us. The same impulse that fashioned starfields from hydrogen and helium molecules, that forged the heavy elements in the furnace of an exploding star, and that moved through a single-celled bacteria on our planet to issue in all the forms of life that we see today also moves through our own self-reflexive consciousness. The new Pentecost will include spiritual practices that tap into this Spirit-animated impulse, and catalyze new structures of consciousness and life practices that will help life on our planet to continue to thrive.

This is already happening. Craig Hamilton, a leader of evolutionary spirituality, just finished hosting a teleseminar series in which he interviewed the world's evolutionary luminaries. By the end of the last program, over eighty thousand people from across the world were listening. This was a language they could relate to and the presence of Spirit was palpable. A Pentecostal community is emerging across the planet. At Canadian Memorial we are attempting to mine historical spiritual practices and create new ones in order to experience in our own bodies, hearts, and mind the power of Spirit in and through this evolutionary impulse. When we identify with this impulse, and live from it, a new, evolutionary Pentecost is possible.

Flaming Love

ACTS 2:1–13

O Holy One,
we gather to rediscover fire—
kindled by an ember that flew from the great radiance,
Love's bright beginning
in time and space—
flaming forth now in us.

May our own Spirit-fanned words
and the thoughts of our hearts
become love's flames,
tongues of forgiveness,
sentences of justice,
declaring the good news:
that Wisdom burns
in the heart of this cosmic adventure.

Pour out a Pentecostal blessing upon us;
transform our babbling into a syntax of blessing,
a proclamation that the world is ablaze with your glory,
that we are suffused in Spirit,
and that all creation is awaiting
our arrival as your sons and daughters—
fire, now shape-shifted into conscious future-forgers—
willing to reveal and realize the kin-dom of God.
Amen.

Glossolalia of Yearning

ACTS 2:1–11

O Holy One,
our prayer is a hunger for wholeness,
an insatiable appetite for completion,
a sighing for coherence.

What is easy to forget
is that you are the Desire of our desires.
You burn within us as the intuition of greater freedom,
of deeper meaning,
of a brighter future,
for us, our families, our communities, and our world.

Today, we honour this "blessed unrest,"[18]
this "divine dissatisfaction,"
as your very image
that flared in Jesus,
leaving him no place to rest his head—or heart.

We open now
to Spirit's fierce push and pull of the possible.[19]
We give thanks
for Spirit-sighs that sound in us,
a glossolalia of yearning
that angels decipher
and translate into choruses of praise.
Amen.

---

18. With thanks to Martha Graham. Agnes de Mille, *The Life and Work of Martha Graham* (New York: Random House, 1991) 264.

19. Thanks to Andrew Cohen. Andrew Cohen, *The Pull of the Possible,* Andrew Cohen's Blog, http://www.andrewcohen.org/blog/index.php?/blog/post/the-pull-of-the-possible.

TRINITY SUNDAY

Many non-Christians and a growing number of "progressive" Christians would just as soon skip all references to the Trinity. The doctrine of the Trinity can be very complex and abstract. But the Trinitarian intuition—that Ultimate Reality constitutes a community and not an individual being—is profound. It also corresponds to what science is discovering.

For the past one hundred years, psychology has assumed an autonomous and independent self that one must "get in touch with" and then bring to relationships. Well, it turns out that this was a wrong assumption. Early feminists correctly noted that the self, a healthy self, comes into being in and through relationships.

At the quantum level of reality, scientists have long ago dispensed with the Newtonian search for the smallest discrete particle as a way of determining the fundamental building block of the universe. At this level it is very difficult to find an isolated anything. Everything exists in relation to everything else, and what's more, everything appears to be everywhere. There's a lot of shape-shifting going on. Reality shows up in either wavelike or particle form, depending upon what the observer wants to measure. The metaphor of the Trinity conveys this quantum insight that, fundamentally, the universe is radically relational.

Ancient Greek theologians had a word that playfully conveyed the communitarian nature of the Trinity: *perichoresis*. It comes from *perichoreuo*, meaning "to dance around." Each of the members of the Trinity is encircling the others in ecstatic dance, a whirling dervish spinning off new worlds born of their joyful play. To wrestle with the doctrine of the Trinity is to celebrate that the entire universe, including humans, emerges out of a relational matrix—a cosmic Trinitarian dance.

This Happy Communion

JOHN 17:20–23

Holiest Mystery,
Community of Love,
Creator, Christ, Spirit,
Three in One,
you in Christ,
Christ in us,
and everywhere, Spirit,
connecting, caressing, cajoling
us into the image of wholeness
tattooed on the heart and the soul
of every living thing.

We are not alone,
never isolated except in the imagination
of our wounded hearts.
Christ abides in us,
and we in Her,
and the joy of this is why we sing,
and why we pray,
and why we take our place
in this happy communion.

Thank you for this banquet of love,
this feast of joy,
this miracle of common purpose
in Christ.
Amen.

The Cosmic Cha-Cha

2 SAMUEL 6:1–5, 12–16; MATTHEW 11:16–19

From the triune communion of Blessed Oneness,
divine joy overflowed into creation.
Love, hidden in fire,
was birthed into becoming
a burning desire
to share the blessed companionship
with creation.

And so Holy Oneness flared forth,
calling electrons and protons into communion,
taking flight on the wings of photons,
primal angels of life,
ever onward,
creating the dance of life.

Spiral galaxies spread their jewelled arms
around space's ever-broadening shoulders,
and together whirled and swirled in a celestial rhythm
that would soon allure our planet onto the dance floor of life.

Now we gather
to celebrate Ancient Wisdom and Cosmic Christ,
and their patient revealing
of the cha-cha within the chaos.

Our bodies and hearts begin to sway
to the rhythms of Spirit,
and to be swept away
in celebration of sacred Mystery.
Holy, Holy, Holy Oneness,
heaven and Earth are indeed full of your glory.
Amen.

SEASON OF EMERGENCE
(ORDINARY SEASON)

This is the long season during which we hear the stories of the life of Jesus and ask ourselves what it means to live out the Christian life in the world. I've called it the Season of Emergence to indicate that in this evolutionary model we don't just ask ourselves "What would Jesus do?" and try to copy him: rather, we allow the heart and mind of the Christ to emerge in us. We are becoming, using the phrase of mystic C.S. Lewis, "little Christs."[20]

The prophet Isaiah challenged his people to trust in a God who was always in the process of doing a new thing: "Do not remember the former things, or consider things of old. I am about to do a new thing. Now it springs forth, do you not perceive it?" (Isaiah 43:18–19).

I define "church" as a domain or habitat for creative emergence. We are together in such a way that we are always seeking the "new thing" God is doing in our midst. For the times we are in, this is critical for a mainline church. Life conditions have changed so drastically that unless we are willing to creatively adapt, our extinction is immanent.

I discuss this in detail in *The Emerging Church*. In an evolutionary paradigm, tradition represents innovations of past generations that have served well in the past and continue to be a source of life. Traditional*ism*—clinging to past forms and processes out of a sense of nostalgia—is a death sentence. We cannot rely on traditionalism in the name of the God in whom new things are always springing forth, and hope to survive.

20.C.S. Lewis, *Mere Christianity* (London: Macmillan, 1960), 166.

Holy Longing

MATTHEW 8:18–22

O Holy One,
you have set us within a world of wonders,
an endless font of fascination.
We are fired into this world
with bottomless desire.

Forgive our fascinations,
which lead us away from the sacred
and toward the profane.

We are mesmerized by violence,
transfixed by displays of dominance,
and allured by the fetish of personal fortune.

Still you do not give up on us.
You are the persuasive pull of love,[21]
and the insistent push
over the edge of yesterday's truth.

You are the message of meaning—
and the promise of love
written into the stars and the life of this planet—
manifest in Jesus,
beckoning truth
and beacon of becoming.
We rest in holy longing.
Amen.

---

21. I am indebted to process philosopher A.N. Whitehead for the image of
persuasive love as distinct from coercive love. A.N. Whitehead, *Adventures
of Ideas* (New York: Macmillan, 1933; Cambridge University Press),
chap. X.

Releasing into Grace

You, O Holy One,
are the cathedral of love,
inviting us to enter and rest
in the sacred space
of your being.

You are the evolutionary urge
sending us out beyond the safety of the sanctuary
into the world
to know you
in and as our own becoming.

You are the measure of our lives,
causing us to know the distance
between our small gestures of love
and the extravagance that is our destiny.

You are the soothing voice reminding us
that you are the lover,
and that we have loved enough.[22]

We release
into the grace of being and becoming,
knowing that you are the nameless one
within both.
Amen.

---

22. With thanks to Leonard Cohen. Leonard Cohen, "You Have Loved
Enough," *Ten New Songs* (Sony Music, 2001).

The Three Faces of God

We gather in this sacred space and time
to remember our face before
we were born,
and before this universe
exploded into forms most glorious.
We open to the ground of being,
the matrix of fecund emptiness.

We gather to gaze upon the mystery of creation,
the beauty and the buzz and the terror
of the natural world,
and to gaze upon your face,
revealed in the great web of creation.

We gather in devotion
to you, our Beloved God and Goddess,
Mother and Father,
Giver of Life,
Wise One and Guide;
you care for each of us with a love
we cannot comprehend
but only humbly receive.
We open and bow before your loving presence.

Before these three faces of our one God,
we find stillness,
surrender to awe,
and fall into Love's embrace.
Amen.

Travellers in Time

Let us gather now,
friends of Spirit—travellers in time—
to hear the story
of Love's evolving narrative.

In this sacred space,
we release into the present,
laying aside all worries, plans, and complaints,
entering into the now
of Mystery's eternal temple.

In this sacred space,
we honour our past,
retelling the great story of deep time
as Spirit's unfolding tale,
giving thanks that a whole universe
is gathered up in the likes of us—
tradition's promise.

In this sacred space,
we consent to the allurement
of an unrehearsed future,
from where the living Word
woos each one of us toward
our unique expression—
that is Spirit's dream.
Amen.

Knit One, Purl Two

GENESIS 37:1–24

We have managed to roll together
the tangled strands of our lives
and get ourselves here.

We take this soft and colourful ball of life—
the school knapsacks filled with anticipation,
the news from home,
the co-worker we can't stand,
the friend that means the world to us,
the dreams that could come true if we just had time,
the failures that haunt our sleep,
the medical report we await,
the love received,
the healing laughter—
we take it all and entrust it as an offering to
the Cosmic Knitter,
who fashions—like an ancient granny—
from these ends of our lives,
a coat of many colours.

We place these woolly bits of our living
in the knitting bag
of this sacred liturgy,
listen for the eternal click and clack of needles,
and eagerly await the finishing touches of Spirit.
Amen.

Spirit Is with Us

JOHN 15:26, ACTS 1:1–5

We gather to renew our confidence
in a more illumined future,
as we enter the kin-dom of God,
here and now
as a foretaste of what is to come.
We give ourselves to this emerging future,
knowing that our choices,
no matter how small,
resonate across every strand of this cosmic web.

We are not alone as future-forgers:
In our fear
that keeps us looking back over our shoulder,
Spirit is with us.
In our passion
to create a holy future,
Spirit is with us.
In our resolve
to face and overcome
all that keeps us from our ideals,
Spirit is with us.

Lift us up, abiding Spirit,
above all obstacles,
and grant us a glimpse
of what is possible
when hearts and minds
discover that you are in our fears,
our hopes,
and our commitments.
Amen.

Hands Opening

LUKE 17:20–21

We gather now
to deepen our trust,
relax our grip on life,
and let go—for one brief hour—
into a matrix of grace.

We witness
the fearful protests of ego
as we imagine
releasing our white-knuckled grip
on life.

Show us the way, brother Jesus,
into the kin-dom of God,
which is always already present
for those who have discovered the
free-fall wisdom of the open hand.
Amen.

Holy One, Holy Oneness

REVELATION 21:1–8

We open now to the mystery of Life,
to the Holy One and Holy Oneness,
infinitely greater than words can express,
and yet the Heart of our hearts,
and the Mind of our minds,
and whose love for us and all creation
exceeds our capacity to imagine.

We open now to the mystery of Life,
to the Holy Oneness,
the web of life that holds all beings
in intimate embrace,
making it possible to distinguish
but never disconnect
any part from the whole,
or whole from the parts,
making us kin
in the kin-dom of life.

We open now to the mystery of Life,
knowing this adventure
to be a journey back to the ever-present source—
discovered in our own depths—
and a forward journey
toward a new heaven and a new Earth,
which is being born through us,
and know above all and below all
that this is not a path to God,
but a path in God.
We celebrate this great adventure.
Amen.

The Pulse of Possibility

ISAIAH 62:3–5

When will we learn,
O Lover of all creation,
that self-diminishment is not a
prerequisite for the Christian life?

You do not ask us to
drag around our sad sack of sins,
raising clouds of dust in our footsteps
for all to see;
and you do not ask us to do one more
wretched thing from guilt—
particularly, serve you.

When will we learn,
O Tender One,
that all you ask is for us to open our hearts
and to love this precious planet
with the love in your sacred heart?

Here, now,
we stop running from the obvious—
we are:
Love enfleshed,
Love wounded,
Love crazed,
Lovesick;
and all that you ask
is for us to stop whatever it is we think we're doing
and be who we are:
a sacred cosmos awakening to itself,
the mind of the planet fetching a new future,
your heart pulsing with possibility.
Amen.

Into the Deep

LUKE 5:1–11, MATTHEW 4:18–22, MARK 1:16–20

Holy Friend,
even as we hear Jesus
inviting us to let down our nets
into the deep waters,
we confess a preference
for the shiny surface of things,
which both fascinates
and fastens us to the material realm.

We easily confuse:
bigger with better,
heaps with happiness,
spectacle with significance,
Hallmark with heartfelt,
consumership with the citizenship,
and net worth with worthiness.

Yet something deep within stirs
as the Nazarene calls to us
to drop our disoriented selves,
like nets,
into the Gennesaret of your being,
teeming with abundant life.

For the joy of it,
we leave behind
our profane confusion
for the sacred simplicity
of awakening to a living universe,
to love,
and to the joy of living within a miracle,
here and now.
Amen.

Chaordic Trust[23]

GENESIS 1, PSALM 19

Come, friends of Spirit,
let us gather in gratitude,
opening to the chaos of life:
the mistakes,
the messes,
and the muddles.

But let us also open
to the order of things—
the magnificent
and the marvellous pattern of it all—
and to beauty that is beyond our minds
to comprehend,
but not to be apprehended by.

Let us calmly celebrate
that we are held
by an order that emerges from the chaos,
and by a chaos that loosens suffocating structures,
and let us learn to trust
that this play of Order and Chaos
is Spirit
dancing its way
into a sanctified future.
Amen.

---

23. *Chaordic* is a term coined by Dee Hock. Dee Hock, *Birth of the Chaordic Age* (San Francisco, Berrett-Koehler Publishers, 2000).

Archetypes of Evolution
COLOSSIAN 1:15–20, ROMANS 8:18–28

We open now to the kin-dom of Life,
even in the midst of death.

We open now to the kin-dom of Beauty,
even in the midst of the marred and the mangled.

We open now to the kin-dom of Goodness,
even in the midst of egocentric foolishness.

We open now to the kin-dom of Truth,
even in the midst of falsehood.

For we know that all things work together for good,
for those who trust the Holy Oneness
and who are called to manifest
the image of the Christ
in word, in deed, and in thought.

We open to the possibility
that in this sacred time together
we may take one small step
toward the beauty, goodness, and truth
known in and through the Christ,
and that we all may open
to these archetypes of evolution.
Amen.

Held Together by Christ

COLOSSIANS 1:17

We gather to give thanks:
for the stillness that renews,
and for the striving that drives us onward;
for the resting in grace, by a lake with a book,
and the blessed unrest that fashions new futures;
for the deep peace of being here and now,
and the wrestling with what's past
for the sake of tomorrow.

We give thanks that the whole of it
is held together by the one we call
the Christ,
that the peace and the struggle of our lives
is not in vain,
but is an offering of love
to this unfolding story of the universe
that we are telling with our lives.
Amen.

When Two or Three Are Gathered, There Is Hope

MATTHEW 18:20

Come friends,
let us walk together in this field of love
that is the ubiquitous presence of the Christ.
Let us gather ourselves in,
and discover
who we are when we are not afraid—
when the universe is known as "Friend."

Yes,
and let us discover who we may become
when just two or three of us
share a common mind and a common heart,
willing to be made over and anew
by the one
around whom the whole cosmos spins
and throws off starfields—
sparks of future possibility
that now shine out from us,
and as us.

Take these stardust forms,
the latent dream of galaxies—
now alive with conscious intent—
and fashion another future
from the radiant field of our collective yearning
for some unimaginable future
that is the dream of those who walk with Christ.
We are witnesses to this kind of love,
this kind of power.
We burn with hope.
Amen.

Again, I Say Rejoice

PHILIPPIANS 4:4–7

Presider: When the sun shines,
           and when the rain falls,

All: we rejoice.

Presider: When the money gods smile upon us,
           and when the bottom falls out of the market,

All: we rejoice.

Presider: When family is the wind beneath our wings,
           and when it is a hurricane of hurt,

All: we rejoice.

Presider: When we are strong in body and mind,
           and when illness reveals our vulnerability,

All: we rejoice.

Presider: When the beauty of creation drops us to our knees
              in awe,
           and when the injustice of humanity drops us to our
              knees in prayer,

All: we rejoice.

Presider: For we are in you,
           and you are in us,
           and there is a country of the soul
           where the eternal joy of Being
           sustains us on this rocky road of becoming.

All: We rejoice and give thanks.
           Amen.

The Mathematics of Abundance

MARK 8:1–10, MATTHEW 15:32–39

Teach us, Sacred One,
the multiplication tables of the kin-dom—
the exponential growth of love shared,
kindness offered, and smiles sewn
in the fields of our daily routines.
Teach us the memorization tricks of the saints,
the algebra of the care-free.

When will we learn the ancient wisdom
that the gods and goddesses of fortune
bow down before
the extravagant ones,
those who risk an open heart,
and the happy-go-lucky?

Teach us, in this time, not to be afraid,
to seed the world with your love,
not to fear a harvest of overwhelming blessing,
to master the mathematics of abundance,
by which seven loaves of bread times a few small fish
equals a feast for the multitude.
Amen.

Sentenced to Hope

REVELATION 21:1–8

O Holy One,
we gather, listening for a word
that is trustworthy and true;
we have had our fill of worthless words,
slick and smooth,
politic and pleasing,
euphemisms and truisms,
none that would pry open our hearts
and cause us to pitch in and help realize
a new heaven and a new Earth.

String together, here, this morning,
a few words that sentence us to hope—
helping us to believe that you dwell with dreamers
who trust that even now you are fashioning,
from tears and terror,
a holy city
where the homeless find shelter
and the heartless find love.

Help us to hear the resonant voice
declaring words of wonder:
that crying and pain will be no more,
that your kin-dom,
eternally present and yet always coming,
is being birthed
through the words of poets,
and the likes of us,
announcing that your dwelling place
is with all creation.
Amen.

Hidden Wholeness

LUKE 9:37–42

Gracious and Holy God,
we gather this morning,
opening to your healing power.
We do not understand all the things
that make us whole,
nor the mystery of all that cripples us
in body, mind, and spirit.

But we do know this:
that the presence of Christ,
the hidden wholeness coursing
through your wondrous universe,
weaves, from the dropped threads of unfinished lives,
a fabric of unmatched beauty.

We come this morning,
seeking less to understand this Healing Source
than to open ourselves
to its sacred flow,
released in us
through this simple act of gathering,
singing, praying, and holding one another
and our beautiful, broken planet
in your love.
Amen.

A Listening Ear

MATTHEW 13:1–16

Let those with ears to hear listen:

O Holy One,
when did we stop listening?
How did we come to believe
that we know everything
that is about to come out of the mouths
of our partners, children, and teachers?

When did the sound of a red-winged blackbird
cease being a source of delight for us?
How did we decide that it is not worth the effort
to enter the world of what is other than us?
When did we stop listening to our own lives
as sources of sacred revelation?
Why did we stop listening to the echoes of the past,
where wisdom stores life's lessons,
or for the strains of that yet-unformed future,
waiting to be born?

Grant to us the robin's focus,
that we might turn our ear—
away from all profane distraction
and listen for the silent, sure stirrings
beneath the surface of things—
as though our life depended on it.
Amen.

An Architect's Eye

GENESIS 6:13–22, JOHN 5:10–16

O Holy One,
faith is an awesome gift:
not that we believe in you,
but that you believe in us!
You have set within us the awesome power of creativity,
entrusting us to shape a holy future.

Within us is the renovating vision of Jesus,
able to enlarge the room we call reality,
replacing walls with floor-to-ceiling windows,
installing skylights to see
the view above our heads.

Respectfully, we remove the ancient symbols
from our sacred table
to spread out the kin-dom's blueprint,
knowing that Jesus is present,
with sharpened pencil
and an architect's eye
for the symmetry of the sacred.

With plans in place,
we take up the hammer
in the spirit of Noah,
carpenter of a divine restoration,
and on behalf of all creation,
we build on your belief in us.
Amen.

Lost and Found

MATTHEW 18:10–14

Holy One,
how long,
how long
until we realize that it is love
which set the stars in place
and binds the planets in their orbits?

How long until we understand that the cardinal's whistle
is a love song,
a canticle of praise for the lover,
and that Earth's long journey through this cosmos
is the time it has taken to awaken to Love's embrace?

How long until we realize that we are here,
not to increase net worth,
but to awaken to our own intrinsic value
as Love's progeny.
You are the hidden heart of the cosmos,
and when we turn our attention to the affairs of the heart,
there we find you,
smiling,
from everywhere and everyone,
joyous to know that another lost soul has been found.
Amen.

Breaking the Silence

LUKE 19:28–40, MATTHEW 21:1–11, MARK 11:1–11

Jesus tells us that even the stones
would cry out if we kept silent.
How do we,
now the stones' vocal chords,
express our awe?

The weight of pink cherry blossoms
drooping against blue sky,
and the return of the yellow and oranges faces
we call "daffodil" leave us speechless.
Even as the word leaves our lips,
it must be followed by a confession
that our naming of things
domesticates the wild mystery of life
and manages the "spell of the sensuous,"[24]
which threatens to stop us in our tracks
and grind the industry of our "getting and spending"
to a blessed halt.

We consent to this Sabbath from certainty,
Holy One,
so that we might be reinitiated into the mystery
of life on this planet,
this blue jewel that came to life—
Love's project—
and came to consciousness in us
so that we might break the stony silence
with praise for you,
whom we've learned to never bet against.
Amen.

---

24. David Abram, *The Spell of the Sensuous* (New York: Vintage, 1997).

The Drop

LUKE 5:1–11

Holy Friend,
we gather this morning
weary and worn from the industry
of our living.

Like the Galilean disciples,
we have been fishing night and day
without a single sardine
to show for our troubles.
We have worked our fingers to the bone,
worried our minds into a fine mess,
and frightened our hearts into hiding.

But it is a new day.
Speak words of grace
into our anxious striving.
Stir us with new purpose,
and grant us a vision
that a soul would want to drop its net into.

Reveal to us the abundance,
the hidden, teeming life,
just below the surface of our
longing lives.

What is there to do but to follow
our beloved,
the depth-finder Nazarene,
with a new determination
born not of our grit
but of your grace?
Amen.

A Blessed Limp

GENESIS 32:22–32

Holy One,
we thank you for not letting us go.
You will not give us over
to whatever it is within us
that contracts
from creation's dream for us.

When we flee, with Jacob, from our past,
you bring it forward,
placing our fears before us,
making them messengers of a grace
that is gained only by wrestling
them to the ground
(or being pinned by them).

When we flee from the present
and escape into distraction, boredom, and busyness,
you call to us from burning bushes,
and the radiance of now.

When we cower in the face of the future,
you beckon us,
beyond the limits of our imagination,
to see with Vision's logic.

How can we thank you
for preferring to go twelve rounds with us
rather than leaving us to fritter away our lives?

As we gather for worship,
we prepare to meet you,
our Loving Challenger,
in the past, present, and future
of our lives,
even if it means leaving with a limp.
Amen.

A Simple Thank-You

LUKE 17:11–19

Most Holy One,
Order within Chaos,
Chaos within Order,
Freedom within Destiny,
Life within Death,
Death within Life,
you are the air we breathe,
the green of trees,
the shape of ferns,
the colour of flowers,
the humming of city streets,
the sound of silence,
the laughter of children,
the weeping of the forlorn,
the longing for peace,
the dream of justice,
the tear of joy
as the arms of our hearts fling open
to the beauty of it all
and our voices utter
a simple thank-you
that changes everything.
Unsolicited praise rises.
Amen.

Hemorrhages and Holy Hems

MARK 5:25–34, MATTHEW 19:18–26, LUKE 8:40–56

Holy God,
we bring an audacious faith,
bold enough to break through
everything and anything
that would keep us from your healing touch.

So much conspires to keep us from reaching out—
beyond our self-conception,
beyond social convention,
beyond the systems that overpromise and under deliver—
to touch into your intention for wholeness.

With the unnamed woman,
hemorrhaging life
yet refusing to suffer in silence,
we reach out to touch the hem of the Christ's garment.
With nothing left to lose,
except a life of isolation,
we choose community,
we choose health,
we choose Wisdom's wish for us,
holding fast to the saving flow of your compassion.
Amen.

The Language of the Soul
ACTS 10:9–16

O Holy One,
we confess that we suffer from tunnel vision.
We find ways to narrow our focus
and fixate on facsimiles of the life you offer,
rather than embracing the real thing.

Too often
we confuse traditionalism for tradition,
theology for direct knowing,
and dogma for the divine.

Drop sheets of sacred possibility
from the heavens,
blanket our consciousness
with unimagined possibility.

Help us to dream, with Peter,
of wide-open hearts and minds,
of bridges that span cultural divides,
of a world liberated for love—
one that is coming into being
through us
and all those who have learned
the dream language of the soul.
Amen.

Shepherd

PSALM 23

Tender God,
we yield to your gentle guidance.
Like a shepherd, you provide all that we need:
you know when we should lie down and rest,
and when we should rise up and be on the move.
Help us to trust the rhythms of the spirit;
lead us away from compulsive action
and the false peace of apathy.

You restore our souls.
We gaze into still waters
and see ourselves clearly now:
reflections of your image
looking back with love.

You lead on the paths that are right for us
and for this planet.
We trust your guidance.
Even in the darkest valleys
and most treacherous passes,
the ground beneath us is firm,
and our confidence is great
that you are with us.

You, Great Shepherd,
the ground of our being,
do not desert us.
Our cup overflows with gratitude.
May our lives be filled with compassion and goodness:
this is all you ask in return.
Amen.

Trinity

We open now to Sacred Mystery,
to the Holy One,
who is infinitely greater than words can express,
and yet is the Heart of our hearts,
and the Mind of our minds,
and whose love for us and all creation
exceeds our capacity to imagine.

We open now to Sacred Mystery,
to the Holy Oneness,
the web of life that holds all beings
in intimate embrace,
making it possible to distinguish
but never disconnect
any part from the whole,
conferring kinship
in the kin-dom of God.

We open now to Sacred Mystery,
to the I Am-ness
that was and is and always shall be
our face before we were born,
before the glorious becoming began.

In devotion, we open to you, Great Thou of all creation.
In awe, we open to the Great Unity.
In humility, we open to the Great I Am.
Amen.

Resting in Love

JOHN 14:18–24

O Holy One,
by your grace
we enter now
the sacred realm,
a place of deep connection
with you,
with each other,
with the planet,
and with all creation.

By your grace,
the walls that isolate fall;
fear dissolves into trust;
arrogance is gentled by compassion;
our need to prove ourselves is tempered
by self-acceptance.
Now, we rest in a love
that helps us see our lives
as part of a great unity,
a coherence of grace.
We join with all creation in
proclaiming your glory,
and the glory of being alive.
Amen.

Only Kisses

LUKE 15:11–32

Holy One,
your love for us is fathomless.
We can neither comprehend it
nor can we ever penetrate its depths.

Yet we insist on measuring ourselves
by the worst in us,
by the slipups and the shame-filled moments.
Release us from our worn-out scripts,
which imprison us,
lock up life,
and leave us languishing in death.

You call us from disgrace to dignity,
and await the return of our prodigal souls
with outstretched arms,
a royal robe,
and the finest champagne:
instead of lessons to put us in our place,
you adorn our faces with kisses,
reminding us who we are
in your welcoming eyes.
Amen.

The Light of Spirit

EPHESIANS 5:8–14

O Holy One,
we long to open our hearts to you,
to love you with all that we are,
all that we have,
and all that we are becoming
by your grace.

Help us to be unafraid;
help us take refuge in your promises
rather than in rigid principles.
Help us to take solace in your mercy
and not in medicating our mistakes.
Help us to take courage in Christ-like vulnerability,
not in the arrogance of coercion.

In this sacred time,
by the tender encouragement of Spirit,
may the door of our hearts
open just enough
to remember what it's like to trust,
to allow Spirit light
to illumine
and lead us back to you.
Amen.

Rainbow Covenant

GENESIS 8:20–9:17, LUKE 16:19–31

We gather now
to declare,
with the repentant God of Genesis
(the colours of the first rainbow
still dripping from Her brush),
"Never again."

We gather under this prism of penitence,
cosmic reminder
of all that must elicit from us
this sacred mantra:
"Never again."

Never again, to the xenophobic fear
that issues in a holocaust.

Never again, to the colonizing arrogance
that causes another species to disappear forever.

Never again, to the pursuit of private gain
while Lazarus and his children
sit hungry outside our gates.

Never again, to the world's way
of transforming suffering into violence.

May we be a rainbow people,
joining with God in keeping
this ancient covenant,
living the promise
of a new creation
being born through us.
Amen.

The Nameless Flow

O Holy One,
ineffable and yet as near as now.
You are the nameless one,
though named by many traditions.

You are holy,
you are wholeness,
you are that mystery,
that magnificence
that no single tradition can contain.

Your beauty astounds,
your wisdom clarifies,
your abundance flows out
by many rivers
and returns to your ocean heart.

We honour each river—
veins of tradition,
arteries of life,
returning to your fathomless heart,
and back out again into the body of creation.

We are carried away,
trusting the flow
more than our names.
Amen.

SEASON OF CREATION

I am privileged to be part of a team in my denomination that is charged with the responsibility for formally adding a new season into our liturgical calendar: the Season, or the Time, of Creation. Many congregations, such as the one I serve, have already been setting aside four to six weeks of the year for the explicit celebration of creation. This is a time to realize and celebrate that we live within a miracle—life on the planet Earth. As we realize that we are biologically and spiritually kin with all creation, a fierce resolve rises up to defend and protect creation—from ourselves! This means that an ecological mission focussed on the repair of the planet, and living in right relationship with all species, will emerge as a priority, alongside social justice. In truth, ecological and social justice cannot be separated.

Our task as Christians is less to be good stewards of creation than it is to take our proper place in the ecosystem of the planet. Stewardship language may inadvertently (or, indeed, intentionally) leave in place the illusion that we alone, of all God's creatures, are made in God's image, and therefore Earth belongs to us. The realization that we belong to Earth means that we are not so much her beneficent caretakers as we are grateful and indebted members of a single Earth community. We are indebted and grateful because all of our life energy is derivative—a gift of the planet and her species—and the amount of energy we require for our daily functions, let alone extravagant consumption, is enormous. This is a season to regard all creation as a radiant manifestation of Spirit, and to understand that the one we call the Christ is cosmic in scope and in love. All of creation lives and moves and has its being within the heart of the Christ, "in whom all things are held together," according to Saint Paul (Colossians 1:15–17). Our vocation is to fall back in love with creation and to treat the planet, her biosystems, and creatures, as we treat our family.

The Thin Filament Within

JOHN 12:23–25, MATTHEW 13:1–7, MARK 4:1–9

Scatter us, O Holy One,
like seed into fertile soil.
Bury us in the loam
of what is yet to come.
Give us the wisdom, Sower of Life,
to learn the delicate art of dying,
again and again,
until we know the difference
between the shell and the seed,
the persona and the soul,
the role and the real.

Crack open our hard shells
and release the thin filament within
that knows to reach for the sun,
Soul's fragile ambassador,
heralding the universe of life,
waiting to emerge.

Draw our greening souls upward,
in love with light,
and drive our roots deep,
allured by sacred darkness.
Grow us.
We consent to your evolutionary grace.
Amen.

The Word Made Flesh

JOHN 1:1–16

O Holy One,
we have been asleep to our true nature.
Awaken us to the mind and heart of Christ within.
Rouse us to the realization that your love for this planet—
sacred orb of life and consciousness—
was confirmed in Jesus of Nazareth,
cosmic coalescence,
love's form and function,
for us and for all creation!

Salt waters coursed through his blood,
fire-forged elements formed his bones and sinews,
ancient bacteria communed in his gut,
billion-year-old-lightning flashes
fired in his neurons.

The Word made flesh,
love incarnate,
mind of God realized,
heart of the Holy manifest.

Help us to fall in love with everything,
to fall into oneness with all that is,
as you did in Christ,
so that everything and everybody
may be known and honoured
as sacraments of the sacred.
Amen.

Humble Homecoming

LUKE 15:11–24

We gather now,
harvesters of an all-pervasive grace,
unexpected benefactors of the deed
to this great and glorious cosmic inheritance.

We, the walking, waking stars,
ablaze with wonder,
imagination,
and hope,
gather to remember three words:
kinship with all that is;
debt that can only be paid forward;
gift, sacred mantra of the humble.

Creation,
the great and glorious sacrifice of abundance,
asks in return—
only—
that we shed our entitled egos
and drop to our knees,
uttering a single, simple prayer
that changes everything:
"Thank you."
Amen.

Turning Aside to See

EXODUS 3:1–22

We gather now, eyes wide open to wonder.
As Moses turned aside to see
the bush ablaze with eternal Presence,
so in this sacred gathering
do we turn aside to see the world
charged with the grandeur and the glory
of indescribable Mystery.

We turn aside to see
the beauty of each other,
the goodness of this life,
and the truth of sacred wisdom that knows:
Earth to be holy;
all creatures to be kin;
the universe to be One;
and Spirit to be a flaring presence,
for all who turn aside to see.
Amen.

Before the Strangeness[25]

GENESIS 3:1–11

Holy One,
we are a sleepy bunch.
Much gets in the way of the wide-eyed wonder
of living inside a miracle:
we struggle to survive;
we are overwhelmed by grief;
we are overburdened by responsibilities;
we are ashamed by failures of love and will;
we are driven by "success"
and frightened by failure.
Wonder-wreckers abound.

Help us in this sacred time
to rest in you,
to let time go by,
to rest in timelessness,
to see our original face
before the strangeness set in
and separated us
from All That Is,
from you,
and from this teeming miracle
of the kin-dom of life on Earth.
Amen.

---

25. Bruce Cockburn, "Isn't That What Friends Are For?" *Breakfast in New Orleans, Dinner in Timbuktu* (Rykodisc, 2007).

Coming to Our Senses

LUKE 15:11–32

O Holy One,
we are an impetuous lot,
demanding that our every whim be catered to,
and allowing desire to lead us down the path of indignity.

We walk upon Earth as the prodigal species,
taking the inheritance of a fourteen-billion-year-old universe
and a five-billion-year-old planet,
and squandering it in dissolute living.

Now, O Source of All Inheritance,
we come to our senses.
Now, O Compassionate One,
we see the error of our ways.
Now, O Forgiver of Foolishness,
we seek to make amends.

Awaken us to a wonder that issues in humility
and drops us to our knees.
Transform our desire into a burning willingness
to reconcile ourselves one with another,
to heal our relationship to other species,
to see life as pure gift,
and to return with an offering of humility
to your awaiting arms.
Amen.

Written on Our Hearts

JEREMIAH 31:31–34

O God, we awaken to you.
We lift our hands and hearts in celebration.
We thank you for all of this,
all of this that you have entrusted to us:
for the earth that feeds us,
and the air that fills us,
for the sun that gives us life,
and the water that overflows our cups.
We thank you for the resurrection
that is today.

And for the new covenant
that you have written upon our hearts—
an inside-out love
which nobody need teach us—
and for wisdom inscribed on
the sacred scroll of our souls,
requiring no rewards or punishment to follow.
Simple reminders will do.

They are everywhere we turn:
in Jesus,
and throughout this wondrous universe—
every body and every thing is a Post-it Note
calling us back to a genetic covenant of love.
Thank you
for being there, and there, and there. . .
Amen.

A Harvest of Quirkiness

PSALM 19

Gracious God,
how can creation sing your praises,
except with the red wings of blackbirds
flashing across blue sky,
and the croak and splash of frogs
playing hide-and-seek in the ponds?

How can the firmament proclaim your handiwork,
except in the wagging tail of a puppy,
and the focussed attention of a toddler
soaking in the wonder of it all?

How can the heavens proclaim your glory,
except through a morning sun rising upon gold-green grass,
lighting up the face of lovers as Earth spins them
once more into a new day?

Your beauty and goodness, O Immanent One,
requires Earth's diversity
and our own wildness,
breaking down—and out of—
the monotony of prescribed patterns,
choosing rather to take our place
in the dancing procession
of differentness,
the variegated life of Christ finding expression
in this body of the church
and the bodies of our kin-creatures.

Make a harvest, O Holy One,
of our quirkiness,
that we might be your radiant presence.
Amen.

A Light Landing

LUKE 12:22–34

Creator Spirit,
out of nothingness—
no thingness—
a cosmos of intricate harmony
and elegant balance emerged.

How is it that we can walk past butterfly wings—
our minds filled with weightier matters—
and not drop to our knees
in reverie?

In this season of summer,
blow us about in the winds of Spirit,
that we might catch a ride and land
on the green leaf of your choosing. . .

There to do nothing more,
and nothing less,
than enjoy the sheer miracle
of being. . .

Alive,
and awake
to the gift of our existence,
and the love that fashions butterfly wings.
Help us to rest in this grace,
Amen.

Living Earth's Wisdom

We tune our ears to the wisdom of Earth.
It is deep prayer, this listening to her cries,
as Spirit's sighs,
too deep for words.

Unborn generations
call to us from the future:
what did you do when the planet
could no longer bear your foolishness
and began to break?

The growl of the grizzly—
caught in the crosshairs
of trophy hunters and policy makers,
who seem to prize extinction—
is a plea for the rights
of all the disappearing ones.

Hear the bawl of the caribou
asking us for room enough to roam
and arsenic-free water to drink.

The cardinal's whistle,
once joy's message,
is now a haunting lament
for the dwindling chorus of songbirds.

The topsoil—living organism and not lowly dirt—
clears its thinning, chemical-burned voice,
and speaks out for the biotic kingdom
teeming within this dark body.

Mother Ocean beckons us to return
to Her womb,
that we might be born anew
and know our salty tears to be Her own.

The willow drops her loving arms
around our shoulders and brushes us with grace,
whispering that it's not too late.
It falls to us, Wisdom's pupils,
to turn this dirge into a dance of the cosmos.

Let those with ears to hear, rise up.
Amen.

REIGN OF CHRIST

Until recently this liturgical season was called Christ the King Sunday. In the interests of inclusive language, this was changed to the Reign of Christ. Even this term has an anachronistic ring to it. But this festival is loaded with significance when understood in light of the social and political context of the early church, and in light of evolutionary Christian spirituality. In the days of Jesus, there was only one king, and that was Caesar. But the early church challenged this claim by affirming that Christ was "Lord," or King. Our origins as a spiritual movement are deeply subversive, and any time we get too cozy with the powers of the world, we need to remember these roots.

Those first Christians had no way of knowing about evolution. Through this new lens, we affirm that this evolutionary unfolding is presided over and infused by a sacred and sovereign presence. The Christ is the persuasive power of love, nudging and wooing all of creation toward its full radiance and potential. Far from being the Godless, directionless, and random process that the new atheists make it out to be, we affirm that this evolution toward deeper expressions of beauty, truth, and goodness is guided by the absolute, noncoercive presence of Love.

Christ Reigning

PHILIPPIANS 2:1–11

Christ, our Brother.
Christ, our Beginning.
Christ, our End.

Known in Jesus,
Word made flesh;
known as Logos,
Hidden Wholeness;
Pattern within the Chaos;
Wisdom, calling from city streets
for justice and compassion.

Christ, beyond all names,
Deepest Mystery,
Depth of Our Own Being,
awaken us, enfold us, impel us
to realize the dream
that is ours to birth.
Amen.

Imagine Integrity

COLOSSIANS 3:1–4, 12–17

Mighty and tender God,
you, the deep within all,
you, the encompassing heart of all,
we enter now into your kin-dom,
your community of wholeness,
a realm of peace.

We bring our hunger,
and the hunger of our world.
We bring our inner stranger,
and the exiled of the world.
We bring our hurting selves,
and the hurting of the world.
We open to healing.

Inspired,
we dare to imagine integrity
in our inner life, our relationships,
our planet, and our political systems.

We dare to imagine the reign of Christ,
Love's Servant,
your heart
for an unfolding cosmos.
Amen.

PRAYERS FOR PEACE

To be in Christ, Paul tells us, is to experience "peace that passes all understanding" (Philippians 4:7). This requires a lifelong spiritual practice. Peace includes, but is more than a state of, inner peace. Authentic peace encompasses how we show in our relationships, with our most vulnerable and authentic self; it includes the practice of kindness and compassion; as well, it involves transforming our social, political, and economic systems in such a way that they serve not only the wealthy but especially the poor and left-behinds.

In an evolutionary paradigm, peace means something different according to the worldview we inhabit. To a warrior consciousness, peace occurs through the conquest of enemies, so that family and tribe members can enjoy security; to a mythic consciousness, peace occurs through adherence to external authority or to scriptural injunctions; to an achievist consciousness, peace is a function of a healthy economy, discovered in financial security and material success; to a "sensitive" (or egalitarian) consciousness, peace means justice and inclusion of all; to an integral consciousness, peace involves honouring all these worldviews, and it requires that we create a place at the table that honours the underlying motivation for all these worldviews and systems in order to negotiate solutions that work for the whole.

Pax Christos

EPHESIANS 1:1–2

Gather us in, Spirit of the Living God.
Gather the warring factions,
within and without,
and bring us bleeding
to the table of peace.

What ancient animal within
crouches in the shadows,
planning the attack,
turning even our loved ones
into enemies?

We take up arms
no less
against ourselves,
enacting atrocities upon our own bodies and souls.

We privilege primal neurons,
hair-triggered for survival,
but know little of the mind of Christ,
synapses of Spirit
that fire a new future,
Pax Christos,
into being.

Yes, gather us in, Spirit of the Living God,
as we shed our dramas of violence
and dare to become
a new creation.
Amen.

The Peace That Passes All Understanding

PHILIPPIANS 4:4–7

We open now
to a peace that passes all understanding,
discovered not only in that rare state
of a still mind
but also in the midst of chaos,
in the disequilibrium of growth,
in the push and pull of circumstance—
and through it all, an awareness
that is not rattled
but rather, deeply curious.

We open now
to a peace that passes all understanding,
in the street-corner prophet
passing out handbills of hope,
repaid with the derision of passersby;
and in the soldier
defending with bullets and bravery
the right of a little girl to go to school;
and in the labour of lawyers
writing policy to save the spotted owl;
and in the priest's choice
to empower a peasant with the Nazarene's legacy.

We open now
to a peace that passes all understanding,
in the solitude of a monk
holding a broken and blessed planet
in constant prayer;
and in the heart of the Christ,
who transforms violence into His own suffering,

abundant life flowing from His wounds
to the hearts of perpetrators
and the likes of us,
who proclaim Him Prince of Peace.
Amen.

Starting with Ourselves

Presider: We open to the possibility of peace,
starting with ourselves.
We commit to being vulnerable
with one other person this day.

All: **Yes, we open to the possibility of peace.**

Presider: We commit to being open to the suffering
of one other being this week.

All: **Yes, we open to the possibility of peace.**

Presider: We consent to having our heart broken open
by injustice this month.

All: **Yes, we open to the possibility of peace.**

Presider: We commit, this year, to resting in the heart of Christ
so that the violence in our hearts may be transformed.

All: **Yes, we open to the possibility of peace.**

Presider: We commit to being the voice of our beloved
and beleaguered planet.

All: **Yes, we open to the possibility of peace,
starting with ourselves.
Amen.**

WISDOM PRAYERS

Thomas Merton, monk and mystic, wrote: "There is in all visible things an invisible fecundity, a dimmed light, a meek namelesseness, a hidden wholeness. This mysterious Unity and Integrity is Wisdom, the Mother of all . . ."[26]

In *Darwin, Divinity, and the Dance of the Cosmos*, I devote a chapter to our long-lost Wisdom tradition. As I researched, I came to agree with scholar Elizabeth Johnson, who writes that Jesus Christ is the human being Sophia became. At least, the writers of the New Testament, including Paul, saw it that way. They used the Sophia tradition as a template by which to reflect on the story of Jesus' life.

Sophia is the feminine personification of the divine (not merely the feminine aspect of divinity). She does everything that Yahweh (the masculine version of the Jewish God) does, but adds a feminine sacred touch. She creates, helps Noah survive the flood, confronts Pharaoh, and journeys with the Hebrews through the wilderness. She loves creation and delights in the human race. It's Her job to help people become friends of the divine. Sophia regards human beings as foolish and in need of wisdom, rather than hopeless. In response, Wisdom prepares feasts and sends Her servants out into the streets to seek and find the foolish and to invite them to a banquet at which they ingest Her ways. Finally, Sophia pitches Her tent and makes Her dwelling place with human beings. She incarnates in Jesus of Nazareth. The one title attributed to Jesus that scholars believe most likely to have originated with him is the child of Wisdom.

---

26. Thomas Merton, *Thomas Merton: Spiritual Master*, ed. Lawrence S. Cunningham (Mahwah, NJ: Paulist Press, 1992), 258.

This recovery of the feminine divine is essential in correcting an almost exclusive emphasis on the masculine nature of God in the Christian tradition. In and through a scientific lens, sacred Wisdom manifests as the evolutionary intelligence inherent in all of Her creatures, including, but not limited to, the human ones.

Blind Bart's Leap

MARK 10:46–52, MATTHEW 20:29–34, LUKE 18:35–40

Open our eyes, O Holy Wisdom,
to what we cannot see,
despite our looking.

Open our eyes, Source of All Truth,
to what we refuse to see,
despite our need.

Open our eyes, Sacred Coincidence,
to the opportunities that pass right before us,
despite our protests of bad luck.

Open our eyes, Alluring Love,
to the future you call us to create,
despite our disbelief.

Show us the way,
that we might shed our sightless selves
like an old cloak
and leap, with blind Bartimaeus,
at the Christ's invitation
to restore our vision.
Amen.

Irrepressible Sophia

WISDOM OF SOLOMON 7:22–30

We open to the Spirit of Sophia,
Sacred Wisdom,
She who pervades all living things
with radiance,
intelligence,
beauty,
and a spirit of kindness.

Gather us in, Sophia,
prepare a feast
for our whole human family
and for all creation,
that we may know we are one,
and that you fill every living thing
with your grace.

Our foolishness has led us astray,
as we choose to eat the bread that does not satisfy
and drink from the cup that entraps us in our isolation.

Breathe upon us your powerful Spirit
and renew us,
that we may be your people.
Amen.

Walking with Wisdom

PROVERBS 8:31

O Holy One,
we come in humility and awe,
waiting on Wisdom,
Holy Sophia,
to reveal to us Her way.

She, incarnate in Jesus,
embodied in cells and centipedes,
woos us with a wink
into an unknown and unknowable future:
except that it shall be delightful,
for She is delighted by creation;
and it shall be beautiful,
for beauty is the path She walks;
and it shall be good,
for She is the irrepressible goodness of creation;
and it shall be just,
for She is outraged by oppression,
of all Her children,
human and other-than-human.

O Holy One,
we turn now from our foolish ways
to walk the path of Wisdom—
lightly, lovingly—upon and as
this beautiful green planet.
Amen.

Sophia's Delight

WISDOM OF SOLOMON 7:27, PROVERBS 9:1–5

We are drawn together by Sophia,
Wisdom of the universe,
nature's intelligence,
embodied in Jesus
and present in all souls
who gather at Her table.

We gather to receive grace to give up our foolish ways,
to walk in Her light,
to delight in creation and in one another,
as Sophia delights in us.

May we open the gates of our souls,
that Sophia may enter,
making us friends of God and one another.
We open to Her transforming power.
Amen.

Word Incarnate

JOHN 1:1–5, BARUCH 3:37

O Immanent One,
Word made flesh,
ever present as Sacred Wisdom in all creation,
in supernovas seeding the universe
with all the elements of life,
in primal lightning sparking life into being
on our beloved Earth,
in our bacterial kin
fixing oxygen levels fit for our lungs,
and in Gaia, Mother Earth,
tending our home with loving care.

We open to you
with humble hearts,
and minds incapable of containing the mystery—
yet with hearts that can hold the wonder,
spilling out everywhere, in every moment,
for those with eyes to see, and ears to hear.

Lift the veil which keeps the radiance at bay,
that we might see in each other's faces
your immanent glory,
and that we might glimpse
the miracle and magic of this holy happening
which is our life.

Yes, liberate us, before another minute goes by.
We are imprisoned by preoccupations
in the windowless cell of fret and frenzy;
end our solitary confinement
so that we might come rejoicing
into the radiant communion of life.
Amen.

Shekinah's Triumph

ISAIAH 62:1–4

Spirit of the Living God,
we have squandered our planet
in pursuit of our own glory:
the glory of wealth,
the glory of status,
and the glorious triumph of the human species.

May we glimpse, in this celebration,
the other glory,
of which the ancient prophet, Baruch, speaks:
Wisdom's presence, luminous in all of creation,
and souls radiant with infinite grace.
Crown us, then, with diadems of the glory
of the everlasting,
freely given to nongrasping hands.

Fill in the valleys, make low the mountains,
make a straight and level path in the wilderness of our souls
for the unending procession of divine Glory,
making its way, of all places,
to the throne of our hearts.
Amen.

Enjoying the Ride

WISDOM OF SOLOMON 7:26–29

O Holy Father and Divine Mother,
from whom all creation emerges,
we bow before you in wonder and adoration.
We marvel that in this past week
we have travelled seven million miles outward
into the mystery of dark space.

Where to, on this ride in our ever-expanding cosmos?
Why here, on Earth,
and now, in this day and age?

We turn to the Christ
to get our bearings
and glimpse a purpose,
but never to lessen the mystery.

We turn to Wisdom,
divine radiance,
to guide us through time's evolving story,
honoured at being chosen
to be both storytellers
and directors in this great drama—
and thankful for this brief
and breath-taking ride
on our hallowed planet.
Amen.

A Year of Living Wisely

BARUCH 3:29–37

We arrive with New Years determination,
and disciplined resolve:
to get off sugar, be more generous, find a new job,
and take the bus more often—
all good intentions, each with its own track record.

Help us to remember, O Holy One,
an intention to walk the path of wisdom this year,
the way of the of the open-hearted sojourner.

We seek gnosis,
a knowing
that our souls awaken
only to projects that are soul-sized—
ones that overshadow the desperate dramas of ego—
like awakening to wonder,
and to our unity with All That Is,
and to seeing the face of Christ
in the stranger, in the exiled,
and in those who are often too close
to see with sacred vision,
especially ourselves.

Soften our determination to *do* more.
Relax our resolve
and release us from the wiles of willpower,
ego's happy servant.
Enrol us in Wisdom's Academy,
to sit as pupils at Her feet,
so that our own might be led
by Sophia,
Lady of Wisdom,
"into the mystic."[27]
Amen.

27. Van Morrison, "Into the Mystic," *Moondance* (Warner Bros/Wea, 1990).

COMMUNION PRAYERS

Since we are indeed the face of evolution, then when we form a procession to receive the bread and cup, we partake as the conscious presence of the evolutionary universe, streaming toward the promise of even greater abundance. As host, the risen Christ allures us toward this promise with exquisite gifts of Earth, the bread, and the wine. Communion is the sacred evolutionary impulse, embodied in these beautiful and broken pilgrims, streaming toward the promise of abundance that our soul recognizes as trustworthy and true.

And let us remember that our bodies, minds, and souls are quite literally concentrated amalgams of the entire 13.7-billion-year cosmic evolution. Therefore, we bring to the table all of God's creation: the ocean that now runs in our bloodstream, the dust of Earth that is now our flesh and blood, the oxygen that our bacterial kin learned to metabolize, the sun's light that our chlorophyll cousins learned to ingest and turn into energy, our reptilian brain that helped us survive, our mammalian brain that taught us empathy and warmth, and, of course, our human kin, the Neanderthals to Einstein—all this we carry, within our own bodies, minds, and souls, to the table. Communion is quite literally a cosmic feast, including all of creation in the celebration. We are drawn forward by the risen Christ, the presence of Sacred Wisdom, activating our imagination and sacred desire.

What we receive in the bread and the cup is, as our tradition has always claimed, the essence of Christ's presence. But in an evolutionary theological paradigm, this is the not only the two-thousand-year-old presence—the Christ known in Jesus of Nazareth. It is also the presence of the Future Christ, who is alluring us to take a step into what is next for us spiritually. Receiving communion is inherently a risky proposition because we are being lovingly persuaded to loosen our attachment to all that we've come to associate with our self—the beliefs, values, assumptions, and worldviews—so that a new self may emerge. We are submitting to the possibility that, with a mouthful of bread and wine, we risk being "born from above," as the writer of John's gospel puts it.

Cosmic Sacrifice

Presider: God is with you.

All: **And also with you.**

Presider: Lift up your hearts.

All: **They are lifted up in sacred celebration.**

Presider: Let us give thanks.

All: **It is right and good to offer thanks.**

Presider: Holy is this cosmos,
whirling, expanding, living, dying,
yearning for abundance and freedom,
imperfect holiness, reaching for a promise of wholeness,
yet always, already a perfect reflection of Spirit.

All: **We come to this table,
awe-struck creatures,
conscious that as we take these few short steps
to the bread and the cup,
the whole cosmos—gathered up in us—
journeys with us, and in us,
into the sanctifying heart and mind of the Christ.**

Presider: As we are dignified in receiving the life of Christ,
O Spirit of our Living God,
so all of creation is lifted up into the heart of the Holy.
We bring to the table our kin:
the bacteria and the lichen,
the moss of forest floors,
the flora and fauna,
the gilled ones of the sea,
and the feathered ones of the air;
we bring the crawling creatures
and the furry mammals.

All: On their behalf, imbued by their natural wisdom,
we come to the table of the Christ,
the one who was in the beginning with you
as sacred creative principle,
the one who is now the love that fills the cosmos
and the one who will always be
the perfection that allures us
from the dream of the future.

We join in the canticle of the cosmos, singing,
Holy, Holy, Holy God,
heaven and Earth are fully of your glory!

Presider: By the sacrifice of a supernova,
Earth was planted with the seeds of its future;
by the sacrifice of our sun,
Earth flowered forth.
By the sacrifice of Jesus—
star child,
Earth's progeny,
son of Mary and Joseph—
a new creation was born.

In Christ incarnate,
a second fireball flared forth,
the radiant potential of love, forgiveness, and compassion.
We are carried in the draft of this explosive event
toward a future that needs us in order to emerge—
the kin-dom of God.

All: We fall silent before this mystery
and our place in it.

[A moment of silence]

All: We offer ourselves,
the church of Christ,
body, blood, heart, and mind,
for this day and age,
and take our place

in this great sacrificial procession of life.
We pour ourselves out
that all of creation may continue its great pilgrimage
into the heart of Christ,
who was, and is, and always shall be,

Our Beloved,
Our Unifying Principle,
Flesh of our flesh, Mind of our mind, Heart of our hearts,
and Soul of our souls.
Amen.

Feasting with All Our Relations

Presider: Spirit is with you.

All: **And also with you.**

Presider: Lift up your hearts!

All: **We lift them in gratitude.**

Presider: Let us give thanks to the font of love,
from which all blessings flow.

All: **It is good and right to give thanks.**

Presider: This Universe, O Holiest One, is the garb of your spirit.
You flared forth in all directions,
birthing and blessing space and time
with fireworks beyond compare.
You clothed yourself in spiral galaxies
and set the neutron stars in your crown of diamonds.

You are the longing within the atoms for communion,
the urge within each molecule for self-expression,
the knowing within each cell of its dignity.

Your being and beauty flows freely into and through
all of creation and this great procession of life,
which we celebrate at this banquet.

All: **We give thanks for Mother Earth,**
your Spirit enfleshed,
giving birth from Her oceans,
carrying nutrients by Her rivers,
inspiring us through the forests,
feeding us from Her soil,
and delighting us with beauty.

We join with the finned ones and the winged ones,
the four-legged ones and ones that crawl upon Earth,
the mountains and trees, clapping for joy,
singing together a canticle of the cosmos:

[The congregation sings]

All: Holy, holy, holy, my heart, my heart adores you,
          my heart is glad to say the words:
          you are the Holy One.

Presider: In the fullness of time, exceptional beings emerged
           to guide us and set our feet upon a right path.
           We open now to their wisdom:

           To the wisdom of Krishna,
           who helps us distinguish illusion from Reality.
           May we dispel the illusion that our current lifestyles are
              sustainable.

           To the wisdom of the Buddha
           who teaches us to reflect on the
           transitory nature of life.
           May we find the grace to let go of our attachments
           to all that is destroying Earth.

           To the wisdom of Chief Seattle and our indigenous peoples,
           who share with us the wisdom of Earth.
           May we feel our kinship with all life.

           To the wisdom of the Jewish prophets,
           who show us there is a time to speak truth to power.
           May we soon find our voice.

           To the wisdom of the Christ,
           who teaches us the subversive wisdom of the silenced ones.
           May we count among the silenced ones our animal friends
              nearing extinction.

           To the wisdom of Mohammed,
           who inspired ecstatic prophets.
           May we release into ecstasy.

           On the feast of Passover,
           Jesus took bread and broke it;
           he said it was like his own body,
           an offering of self

broken, that we might know the ways of peace,
with all creation.

He also took a cup and, after blessing it,
said it was like his blood,
a pouring out of his very being in the service of life,
a self-donation
inspired by the way of the cosmos
(the sun burning four million tons of hydrogen every second
in the service of the great procession of life).

All: **We bless and are blessed by these elements:**
bread, wine, gifts of Earth,
gifts of the cosmic Christ.
In the sharing of this holy meal,
may they become for us sacred reminders
of all that has been offered in this unfolding story,
all the sacrifices necessary to give us life,
to shape and animate our bodies, our minds, and our souls.

Presider: In sharing this meal, we enter into a new covenant,
with you, with all creation, and with one another,
a promise to walk gently upon this planet,
to raise our voice in the service of life,
to love kindness,
and to seek justice.

All: **We proclaim the mystery of our faith:**
Wisdom has come in Christ
Wisdom was crucified
Wisdom will come again and again.

Presider: We become, with Christ,
an evolutionary offering,
in service to the emergence
of your blessed kin-dom.
Amen.

Epiphany

Presider: God is with you.

All: **And also with you.**

Presider: Lift up your heart.

All: **We lift our hearts to God.**

Presider: Let us give thanks to the one from whom all blessings flow.

All: **It is good and right to give thanks.**

Presider: We are thankful for light,
for the great radiance that gave birth to space and time,
to the starfield garlands strewn through space,
to the supernova fireworks in which were forged
the elements for life on Earth,
to our sun that burns itself out
in the service of life
and takes form in a baby's smile,
in the leafy green expanse we call "tree,"
and in the gaze of the gorilla.
We give thanks for the mystery of light.

The light of all lights
radiated in the consciousness of prophets:
Moses and Miriam, Lao Tzu, Confucius, the Buddha,
the swamis of India, Mohammed, Black Elk, and many
others.

All: **When Jesus was born, his light lit our path:**
a path of sacred wisdom,
a path of forgiveness,
a path of evolutionary grace,
a path of compassion for the left-behinds,
a path that makes room for all,
human and other-than-human,
at the banquet of life.
And so we join in a canticle of the cosmos, singing:

[The congregation sings]

Holy, holy, holy,
our hearts, our hearts adore you.
our hearts are glad to say these words:
You are holy, God.

Presider: At his final meal with his disciples,
Jesus broke bread and helped them to understand
that he had given himself as bread for a hungry world:
"This is my body, broken for you."
When the meal was finished,
he helped them to understand
that he had poured himself out completely for the emergence
  of a new humanity:
"This is my blood, poured our for you."

All: May your ever-present spirit bless these gifts
and bless this gathering,
that we may be transformed by his radiance
and become, by a grace beyond our understanding,
the light that shines, first upon those places within ourselves
that are born of fear,
and then those dark places and ways of being in the world
that are the children of fear.

To you,
whose light and love "fires the sun"
and keeps us burning,[28]
we dedicate this banquet of love.
Amen.

---

28. Thanks to Bruce Cockburn. Bruce Cockburn, "Lord of the Starfields," *In the Falling Dark* (True North, 1976).

Christmas Eve

Presider: God is with us.

All: **God is within us!**

Presider: Open your hearts.

All: **Our hearts open to the mystery of this night.**

Presider: Let the heavens rejoice!

All: **Let Earth be glad.**

Presider: O Holy One,
we join with the creatures of Earth,
giving thanks that Earth is your body
and from Her womb, through your beloved servant, Mary,
one was born who showed us the path of humility.

The whole universe:
stars and mountains,
lamas and lions,
flowers and forests,
the angels and the human ones,
all join in a canticle of the cosmos
celebrating this enfleshing miracle—
your incarnation
in Christ and through this evolving miracle of life.

All: **Holy, Holy, Holy God,**
Earth is full of your glory!
In this sacred Bethlehem birth
we are reminded that we are called
to give birth to the Christ in our age.

Presider: In Jesus, your intention
to carry all creation into wholeness
pulls us along.
We come to know your love

as a holy alluring to be, for this planet,
the presence of love.

The Word made flesh
gathered with his friends for a final meal,
a last reminder that he was the very heart of God,
symbolized in bread and wine,
broken and poured out so that we might find our way
back to your heart.

All: You, O Holy One, are blessed.
          You, O Holy One, are good.
          You, O Holy One, are gracious.
          You, O Holy One, are always blessing,
          always birthing, always becoming.
          All praise and honour and glory are yours.
          Amen.

Feast of the Cosmos

Presider: God is with you.

All: **And also with you.**

Presider: God is within you.

All: **And also within you.**

Presider: Let us lift up our hearts and give thanks to our God.

All: **It is right and good to do this.**

Presider: God of this vast cosmos,
Incarnate Love,
garbed in a blue-green mantle,
a floating pearl
of great price,
we give you thanks.

Formed and forged in the expanding shell
of this evolving universe,
your body—our planet—broke open
five billion years ago,
spilling out lava-life, steam, bacteria,
and the prodigious procession of life,
opening, always opening, toward the novel next.
Our cup runs over.

This cup of abundance is held up by our Teacher,
who emerged, like all, from the womb
of this planet,
Mary-shaped now.
We hear his words for our day:

"This is my body,
assembled over vast stretches of time
by the kin-doms of life straining toward perfection:
this body of bodies,
broken now by fear and ignorance

but soon to be transformed by my 'yes'
into an offering
for the new creation the sacred one is birthing.

"And this is my blood,
formed by light rivers of galaxies
running toward and emptying into
the sea of Being that coalesced into this vessel of mine,
now poured out for you,
and pouring into you,
fire of a new emergence—
bright and burning love of my sacred heart."

All: Melt us, O Holy One,
so that a new creation might be born
from our own lava-lives and we may finally put away the
    childish things
that keep us from knowing that your love is maturing
in the most unlikely of places—
in those of us gathered for this cosmic feast.

Help us to sell all we think we possess
so that we may lay claim to the one thing
worth possessing: your wisdom,
embodied in a sacred planet,
the heart of Christ, crucified,
and the resurrected body of Christ,
alive and well,
in this community.
Amen.

Transformation

We give you thanks, Great Transformer.
You are the power
that turns helium and hydrogen
into starfields,
and exploding stars into building blocks of life.
You are the intelligence that, through deep time,
turns lava into llamas,
and bacteria into Beethoven's symphonies.

At the Cana wedding,
Jesus turned water into wine,
the miracle being not the transformation
(for this is your signature),
but the time it took—
the wink of a mother's eye.

And so we know, Holy One,
that in your hands, by your power
and according to your will,
we too may be transformed,
and learn again
that you have saved the best in us
for last.

We come to this table,
incarnating in our own blood and bones,
in chemistry and consciousness,
this shape-shifting universe.

As we receive this bread and this cup—
symbols of self-giving love
and of the mind of a man
who knew that death
is form's portal into Love's formless embrace—
we open to our own conversion

into servers of a rare vintage—
Abundant Life Reserve—
in the crystal glass of Christ's heart.
Amen.

SACRAMENT OF BAPTISM

These days, it's important to keep in mind that the human species—at least those of us in the developed countries who have been living in and through an industrial worldview—have never been more alienated from our connection with Earth. The sacrament of baptism, therefore, needs to be a reinitiation into the matrix of a living universe and the one Earth community. It remains, of course, an initiation into the church, but this is a church that itself needs to be baptized back into a relationship with "all our relations," as the First Peoples teach. In baptism we undergo a death—we die with Christ when we are symbolically immersed under the water—in order to be raised with Christ as a new creation and *with* all creation.

The ritual would do well to incorporate a question about the purity of our baptismal water. What does it mean to baptize with water in a world where there is no longer a pristine body of water on the planet?

The baptismal questions we ask our candidates (or their parents) are explicitly evolutionary and ecological. Are they willing to *be* the new creation we are proclaiming? Is the congregation willing to be a domain of creative emergence that will produce practices and processes that do not impede the natural spiritual evolution of the candidates? Will we as a community and will the candidates (or their parents) walk lightly upon the planet and seek to live in right relation with all kin—human and other-than-human? Baptism needs to become a sacrament of coming home to the cosmos—an awakening to our radical interconnectedness with all of life.

Drenched

We open
to the patient presence of Spirit,
waiting for willing souls—
future-fashioning artists—
to share with Her
a palette of possibility;

waiting, for fourteen billion years,
for us to take up the brush
and daub and dab
new colours—our true colours—
onto the unformed canvas
of the future;

Spirit waiting
for this moment to arrive,
to plunge those with ears to hear
into the waterfall of grace,
shrieking with laughter and delight
under thundering baptismal waters.

Baptise us once more in the spirit,
so that our bold strokes
may draw a wider circle
and play a part in
describing our universe.
Amen.

A Baptism of Belonging

Baptise us all, O Holy One,
into a new way of being,
a new humanity,
fit for the glory and dignity
of this one Earth community.

Blend with these baptismal waters
our tears for all that we have done,
and left undone,
all those we have left behind
and left unloved.

Drown us in the deep awareness
of the kin-dom of God,
of our radical belonging—
in you, with each other,
and with all creation.

Raise us up,
a new creation gasping for life,
that we might grasp the full extent
of the mystery of being—
Alive! Creative! Compassionate!

Now we die with Christ,
that we might also be raised up with Christ,
to throw our arms around this wondrous planet
in a holy and healing embrace.
Amen.

SPECIAL OCCASIONS

Remembrance Day Prayer

O God,
whose heart is broken
by the violence in the human race,
forgive us that we have lacked
the imagination and collective will
to create a warless world.

Forgive us for breaking faith
with those who gave their lives,
for the unconscionable gap between the rich and poor,
for corruption and deceit in high places,
for the profit gained by the sale of weapons,
for the spirit of domination in our world leaders,
for learning so little from the deaths of 100 million
in the past century.

In you alone is our hope;
in your power, which can purify the human heart
and set our feet upon the path of peace, do we trust.
You can do great things
in willing hearts.
Break, then, our hardened hearts.
Break them with grief, with memory, and with hope.
In the name of the Prince of Peace.
Amen.

Prayer for Mothers

O Holy One,
we know you
in the fierce love of a mother
for her children,
in acts of tender care at times of illness,
in the voice of encouragement,
and in times of self-doubt.

We learn something of your love
in the long-suffering love of mothers
for children who have lost their way,
in forms of love that may persuade
but never coerce.

We know you on this Mother's Day
as we remember Julia Ward Howe,
who rose up against injustice
and the carnage of war.

We know you as we give thanks
for Mother Earth,
from whom and through whom
all of your blessings flow.
Amen.

The Lord's Prayer
(ARAMAIC TRANSLATION)[29]

Loving Presence, luminous in all creation,
hallowed be your name.
Thy kin-dom come.
May we reflect on Earth
the yielding perfection of the heavens.
Help us to receive an illumined measure from Earth this day.
Forgive us when we trespass against others,
human and other-than-human,
as we forgive others who trespass against us.
Keep us on the path of wisdom
when we are tempted to take the selfish path.
May it be your rule we follow,
your power we exercise,
and your radiance that allures.
May this be the truth that guides our lives,
the ground from which our future will grow,
until we meet again.

---

29. Thanks to Neil Douglas-Klotz whose book *Prayers of the Cosmos* and his
   original translation inspired and informed this one. Neil Douglas-Klotz,
   Prayers of the Cosmos (Toronto: HarperCollins Canada, 1990).

Works Cited

Abram, David. *The Spell of the Sensuous*. New York: Vintage, 1997.

Angus Reid Strategies. "Creation Museum Opens: Do Canadians Believe in Evolution or Creationism?" Angus Reid Strategies. http://www.angus-reid.com/uppdf/ARS_Evo_Cre.pdf.

Beck, Don and Christopher Cowan. "Spiral Dynamics Gateway." National Values Center, Inc. http://www.spiraldynamics.com.

Bohm, David. *The Essential David Bohm*. Edited by Lee Nichol. London: Routledge 2003.

Brown-Taylor, Barbara. *Leaving Church: A Memoir of Faith*. New York: HarperCollins, 2007.

Cockburn, Bruce. "Closer to the Light." *Dart to the Heart*. True North, 1994.

———. "Isn't That What Friends Are For?" *Breakfast in New Orleans, Dinner in Timbuktu*. Rykodisc, 2007.

———. "Lord of the Starfields." *In the Falling Dark*. True North, 1976.

Cohen, Andrew. "The Pull of the Possible." Andrew Cohen's Blog. http://www.andrewcohen.org/blog/index.php?/blog/post/the-pull-of -the-possible.

Cohen, Leonard. "You Have Loved Enough." *Ten New Songs*. Sony Music, 2001.

Crossan, John Dominic. *Jesus: A Revolutionary Biography*. San Francisco: HarperSanFrancisco, 1994.

cummings, e.e. "i thank you God for this amazing day." *XAIPE: Seventy-one Poems*. Oxford, Oxford University Press: 1950.

Darwin, Charles. *The Origin of Species by Means of Natural Selection*. London: John Murray, 1888.

de Mille, Agnes. *The Life and Work of Martha Graham*. New York: Random House, 1991.

Dickinson, Emily. "Bustle in a House." *Poems by Emily Dickinson.* Edited by Thomas Wentworth Higginson and Mabel Loomis Todd. London: Little, Brown, 1912.

Douglas-Klotz, Neil. *Prayers of the Cosmos.* Toronto: HarperCollins Canada, 1990.

Gebser, Jean. *The Ever-Present Origin.* Athens, OH: Ohio University Press, 1985.

Harvey, Andrew, trans., *Light upon Light: Inspirations from Rumi.* New York: Jeremy P. Tarcher/Penguin, 1996.

Hock, Dee. *Birth of the Chaordic Age.* San Francisco: Berrett-Koehler Publishers, 2000.

Koestler, Arthur. *The Ghost in the Machine.* London: Hutchinson, 1967.

Lewis, C.S. *Mere Christianity.* London: Macmillan, 1960.

Merton, Thomas. *Thomas Merton: Spiritual Master.* Edited by Lawrence S. Cunningham. Mahwah, NJ: Paulist Press, 1992.

Morrison, Van. "Into the Mystic." *Moondance.* Warner Bros/Wea, 1990.

Newport, Frank. "On Darwin's Birthday, Only 4 in 10 Believe in Evolution." Gallup. http://www.gallup.com/poll/114544/Darwin-Birthday-Believe -Evolution.aspx.

Teilhard de Chardin, Pierre. "My Fundamental Vision." 1948.

Whitehead, A.N. *Adventures of Ideas.* New York: Macmillan, 1933; Cambridge University Press.

———. *Process and Reality*, Corrected Edition. New York: Free Press, 1978.

Wilber, Ken. "Toward a Comprehensive Theory of Subtle Energies." Shambhala Publications. http://wilber.shambhala.com/html/ books/kosmos/excerptG/part1.cfm.

Index of Scripture

About the author

Bruce Sanguin has been an ordained minister for twenty-five years, and for fourteen years he has served Canadian Memorial United Church and Centre for Peace, in Vancouver, B.C., Canada. This community has an explicit mission to teach and practice evolutionary Christian spirituality.

Sanguin is also the author of *The Emerging Church: A Model for Change & a Map for Renewal*; *Darwin, Divinity, and the Dance of the Cosmos: An Ecological Christianity*; and *Summoning the Whirlwind: Unconventional Sermons for a Relevant Christian Faith*.

Visit Bruce Sanguin at IfDarwinPrayed.com.

LaVergne, TN USA
11 November 2010
204544LV00002B/2/P